Meredith Westfall and John McCarthy

"Great Debates"

Language and Culture Skills for ESL Students

Illustrations by Renee McCauley

The University of Michigan Press

Ann Arbor

Contents

To the Teacher

This textbook is intended for intermediate-level English learners in high school, college preparation, and adult education ESL programs. The book contains activities in which students discuss the two opposing sides of an issue. We have tried to choose issues that will interest the students and promote discussion in addition to adding an element of fun to the class. In order for students to learn discussion techniques in a relaxed atmosphere, we have avoided controversial or sensitive topics. When using this book, it's important to keep in mind that in debates, we must pick a side and argue for that side and that arguing for one side doesn't necessarily mean one side is good and the other is bad.

Each discussion activity is set up so that all students are engaged in the particular task at hand. All of the debates have **Conversation Tips** and **Language Learning Tips** that are recycled throughout the book. Students are encouraged to use these to facilitate their discussions. In addition to discussion activities, the book contains activities for reading, writing, and vocabulary building.

For each chapter of the book, the format is the same, consisting of the following sections.

Starting Off: Four discussion questions to get the students talking about the topic of the chapter. This section will also allow the teacher to assess the students' prior knowledge on the subject.

Vocabulary: Five new vocabulary words with definitions in English. For each word, there are also two sample sentences showing the word in context. We have chosen the vocabulary items in this book with two different goals in mind. First, we wanted to introduce students to high-frequency vocabulary with which they may not be familiar yet. Second, we wanted to provide students with vocabulary that relates specifically to each chapter topic, so that the students will be able to more fully participate in the discussion activities. An appendix containing all of the vocabulary items appears at the end of the book.

Reading: A two-paragraph reading about the topic of the chapter, outlining the two sides of the issue. Again, the five new vocabulary words appear in context.

Comprehension Questions: Four questions, two for each paragraph of the reading

Discussion Activities: Three activities, including one main activity involving a discussion of the two sides of the issue. The debate activity in each chapter incorporates two expressions used in certain speech acts, for example, agreeing, disagreeing, asking for more information, giving more information, and disagreeing and adding your own opinion. Each chapter also includes one expression related to language learning. A list of all the expressions is provided at the beginning of the book.

Write about It: Three questions related to the topic and intended to be used for writing assignments

People Say: Two idioms or sayings related to the topic

Vocabulary Review: Fill-in-the-blank questions about the five vocabulary words introduced in the chapter

While creating this book, we have kept in mind that every classroom is unique and that teachers may vary in the approaches they use to meet the needs of their students. We hope that teachers will feel comfortable supplementing the lessons with their own ideas and activities if they so choose. Although some of the chapters build on vocabulary from previous chapters, teachers should not feel pressured to rigidly follow the order of the units. Our ultimate goal is to provide the teacher with flexible material that allows students to freely discuss a wide variety of topics and to enjoy doing so.

Conversation Tips

How to Agree

I agree.

That's right.

Exactly.

That's for sure.

How to Disagree

I disagree.

I don't think so.

That's not what I think.

That's not the way I see it.

How to Ask for More Information

Can you explain that?

What do you mean exactly?

Could you give me an example?

Could you be more specific?

How to Give More Information

What I mean is . . .

For example, . . .

In other words, . . .

What I'm trying to say is . . .

How to Disagree and Add Your Own Opinion

I know what you're saying, but . . .

That may be true, but . . .

I see what you mean, but . . .

That's a good point, but . . .

Language Learning Tips

How do you spell that?

Could you spell that for me?

Could you say that again?

Could you repeat that?

What does _____ mean?

What's the definition of _____ ?

How do you pronounce _____ ?

How do you say _____ ?

Could you speak more slowly?

Would you mind saying that again more slowly?

The Debates

1

Dining In or Eating Out?

Starting Off

1. How often do you dine in?

2. How often do you eat out?

3. How much time do you spend preparing your meals?

4. When you eat out, how much do you usually spend on a meal?

Vocabulary

hectic—(adjective) busy, rushed

> For many people, the work week is very **hectic,** so they don't have time to get everything done.

> Bob's schedule was so **hectic** that it took him three months to schedule an appointment for a haircut.

trend—(noun) the way a situation is changing or developing

> The clothing **trend** changes from season to season.

> Many fashion **trends** start in famous cities, such as Paris or Tokyo.

retailer—(noun) a person who sells things

> **Retailers** always hope to make a lot of money during the holidays.

> If it rains too much at a summer resort, it is possible that **retailers** in surrounding towns will lose money.

consumer—(noun) a person who buys things

> Many **consumers** at the supermarket expect good service and low prices.

> **Consumers** don't like to spend too much money on the necessities that they buy.

ingredients—(noun) types of food needed to make a particular dish

> The **ingredients** in cookies include flour, sugar, and eggs.

> Because she is allergic to eggs, she needs to read the label to check the **ingredients** very carefully if she eats any processed food.

Reading

As life becomes more **hectic** and time becomes more of a commodity, people are choosing to eat out more and more. Time they would have spent on preparing food at home can be spent out with family or friends. According to the National Restaurant Association,* Americans ate 4.2 meals away from home each week in 2001. This is up from 3.8 meals per week in 1991. Who works in the food-service

---

* Statistics from http://www.restaurant.org/research/index.cfm, accessed January 20, 2003.

industry? Believe it or not, more than 8 percent of the U.S. workforce is employed in some sort of food-related business. If the current **trend** continues, the workforce numbers will only increase. Everyone loves the restaurant experience when it includes spending more time with friends and experiencing new tastes.

▶ ▶ ▶ ▶ ▶ ▶ ▶

Eating out is a lot of fun, but for some people, making meals at home is an enjoyable way to spend leisure time. There have been a number of cooking shows that have become very popular, and because of this, there are a number of celebrity chefs who are as famous as movie stars or singers. Supermarkets have also been experiencing a recent boom. Supermarkets are offering all kinds of services, from banking to shoe repair and dry cleaning to filling prescriptions. **Retailers** realize that **consumers** are pressed for time, so the additional services have been offered. People who prepare their own meals may have to spend time doing it, but they can choose the **ingredients** they want and create healthy, inexpensive meals.

Comprehension Questions

1. How many meals does the average American eat away from home?

2. How many meals were eaten away from home in 1991?

3. What percentage of the workforce is employed in the food-service industry?

4. What are some services that supermarkets offer the consumer?

Discussion Activities

Activity 1

In a small group, discuss the advantages and disadvantages of dining in and of eating out. In the chart that follows, write down as many ideas as you can think of for each topic.

Advantages of Dining Out	Disadvantages of Dining Out
Advantages of Eating In	Disadvantages of Eating In

It is Friday night, and Rachel has had a busy week at work. Because she has been so busy, she hasn't had time to see two of her close friends. She can't decide if the three of them should go out for dinner or if she should make dinner at her apartment and invite them over. The class will form two groups and debate. Group A will try to convince her to go out to dinner with her friends. Group B will try to convince her to stay home and invite her friends over for dinner. Make sure everyone participates in the conversation.

Conversation Tip

When you want to show that you agree with someone, you can use these expressions:

I agree.

That's right.

A: Going out to dinner after a long week is so much fun.

B: **I agree.** My husband and I love to go out to eat whenever we get a chance.

Language Learning Tip

When you aren't sure how to spell a word, you can use this expression:

How do you spell that?

A: If you want good Italian food, you should go to La Trattoria.

B: **How do you spell that?**

A: You spell it L-A T-R-A-T-T-O-R-I-A.

Try to use these tips in your discussion.

Wrap Up

Which group was more convincing?

What were the strengths and weaknesses of each team's presentation?

Activity 2

Look at the following situations. In each case, decide which would be better, dining out or eating at home.

Be ready to explain your answers.

Situation 1

You are going out on a first date.   Eat in _____   Dine out _____

Situation 2

Your friend from elementary school is   Eat in _____   Dine out _____
coming into town.

Situation 3

Your brother, who you haven't seen   Eat in _____   Dine out _____
for two months, wants to have dinner
with you.

Situation 4

It's a big holiday, and relatives want to   Eat in _____   Dine out _____
spend it with you.

Activity 3

Work with a partner and plan the perfect dinner.

What kind of food would you eat?

Appetizer _____

Main dish _____

Dessert _____

Beverage _____

Would you dine out or eat in for this meal? Why?

Write about It

1. Describe the last meal you ate away from home.

2. When you cook, do you use a cookbook? Why or why not?

3. What is one dish you would like to learn how to make? Why?

People Say . . .

> *A full Belly makes a dull Brain.* —Benjamin Franklin, American philospher and statesman

> *Skinny cooks can't be trusted.* —Saying

What do these sayings mean?

Do you know of similar sayings?

Vocabulary Review

1. If we want to bake chocolate chip cookies, we have to buy the

   _____ at the supermarket.

2. The fashion _____ this season is to wear platform shoes and very

   short skirts.

3. _____ generally spend a lot of money before big holidays.

4. After a _____ week at work, Carol decided to stay home all weekend

   so she could relax.

5. _____ like to display their products in an attractive way, so that

   people will buy more than they were planning to.

Famous or Anonymous?

Starting Off

1. Who are some of your favorite famous people?

2. Why would someone want to be famous?

3. How could someone become famous?

4. What are some bad points about being famous?

Vocabulary

audience—(noun) people who watch or listen to a performance or movie

The movie was very sad, so most of the **audience** was crying.

That band is very popular. Whenever they have a concert, there's always a huge **audience.**

follow—(verb) pay attention to

I don't **follow** baseball at all. I have no idea which teams are good this year.

My father **follows** the news. In fact, he reads two newspapers every day.

anonymous—(adjective) unknown, not connected to a name

Usually, everyone knows that movie star. When she wants to be **anonymous,** she wears sunglasses and a big hat.

I received an **anonymous** birthday card. There was no name written inside, so I don't know who sent it.

recognize—(verb) see someone's face and know who that person is

Susan and Mark hadn't seen each other for 20 years, but she **recognized** him because he still looked the same.

I saw a movie star downtown yesterday. At first, I didn't **recognize** her, because she was wearing sunglasses and a big hat.

autograph—(noun) a famous person's written name

When I saw the movie star, I asked for her **autograph.** She wrote it on a piece of paper and gave it to me.

If you have a very good baseball player's **autograph,** you might be able to sell it for a lot of money.

Reading

Can you think of anyone who became famous overnight? Maybe you know of a singer who performed for small **audiences** and then suddenly had a hit song that millions of people heard on the radio. Perhaps you've heard of an athlete who trained for many years at a sport that few people **follow** and who then won an

Olympic medal and became a national hero. In only a few days, these people went from being **anonymous** to being famous.

▷ ▷ ▷ ▷ ▷ ▷ ▷

When someone becomes famous, his or her life changes greatly. The person's picture is in the newspaper and in magazines. He or she appears on TV talk shows and in commercials. This can make the person rich—and popular. Everyone wants to have a famous friend. Wherever the famous person goes, people **recognize** him or her. They want to talk with that person and get his or her **autograph.** Some stars like this attention, but others would rather not be bothered. They might feel that their life was better before they became famous. How do you feel? Would you rather be famous or anonymous?

Comprehension Questions

1. How can a singer become famous overnight?

2. How can an athlete become famous overnight?

3. How can a famous person become rich?

4. What might happen when a famous person goes out?

Discussion Activities

Activity 1

In a small group, discuss the advantages and disadvantages of being famous and of being anonymous. Write your answers in the chart that follows.

Advantages of Being Famous	Disadvantages of Being Famous
Advantages of Being Anonymous	Disadvantages of Being Anonymous

Grant is a police officer in New York City. He has arrested many criminals and helped many people out of dangerous situations. A movie producer heard about Grant's story and now wants to make a movie about it. The producer has two ideas. The first one is to make a movie starring Grant as himself. If the producer does this, Grant will get paid a lot, and there is a good chance that he will become famous. The second idea is to use another actor and not use Grant's name in the movie. If the producer does this, Grant will still make a lot of money, but he will probably not become famous. The class will form two groups and debate. Group A will try to convince Grant that he should star in the movie. Group B will try to convince him that the second option would be better. During the activity, make sure that everyone has a chance to speak.

Conversation Tip

When you want to show that you disagree with someone, you can use these expressions:

I disagree.

I don't think so.

A: I think it would be great to be a famous movie star.

B: **I disagree.** I would hate to have people bothering me all the time.

Language Learning Tip

When you don't understand what someone has said, you can use this expression:

Could you say that again?

A: I think there are a lot of advantages to being anonymous.

B: **Could you say that again?**

A: I said that I think there are a lot of advantages to being anonymous.

Try to use these tips in your discussion.

Wrap Up

Which group was more convincing?

What were the strengths and weaknesses of each group's presentation?

Activity 2

Have you ever met anyone famous? Talk about this topic in a group of three, but don't let your other classmates hear the discussion. Everyone in the group should tell one story. If you've met someone famous, tell your classmates about how you met that person. If you haven't met a famous person, talk about a famous person you would like to meet and how you might meet that person. In your group, choose one story that you think is interesting. The other groups will have to guess whose story it is, so don't choose a story that they can guess easily.

After you have chosen the story, talk together with your group. Try to imagine what questions the other groups will ask to find out whose story it is, for example, "When did you meet the person?" or "What did you say to the person?" Talk about how you will answer these questions. The people in your group don't have to all give the same answers.

Once you have prepared, the teacher will pick a group to go to the front of the room, and each member of the group should say the same thing, for example, "I met the president of the United States." The other groups can then ask questions about the story. The teacher will ask those groups to guess whether the story they heard was true or false. Next, the teacher will ask the groups to guess whose story it was. A group gets a point for each correct answer. When all the groups have told their stories, the group with the most points wins.

Activity 3

Part 1

The teacher will put a sign with the name of one famous person on every student's back. (Some examples of names for the teacher to use appear at the end of this chapter. The students should not look at these examples until they have finished the activity.) After all of the students have their signs, they should get up and walk around the classroom. Each student will be able to read the other students' signs, but not his or her own. Students should find a partner and look at the partner's sign. Then the partner must ask three questions to try and guess which famous person he or she is labeled as. All questions must be yes-no questions, for example, "Am I a man?" or "Do I play basketball?" After these questions are answered, the other person should ask three questions. At any time, one of the partners can ask, for example, "Am I Michael Jordan?" After each partner has asked three questions, the two students should find other partners. When students know who they are labeled as, they should continue to walk around and answer the questions of their classmates.

Part 2

After everyone knows who he or she is labeled as, each student should find a partner. Each pair should then write a dialogue in which the famous people they are labeled as meet for the first time. They should then read the dialogue to their classmates.

Write about It

1. Suppose you were famous and won an award. If you had one minute to make a speech on TV during the awards show, what would you say?

2. When people are asked to name a hero, they often pick a famous person, such as an athlete or a politician. What kind of person do you think of as a hero? Describe one such person.

3. Describe an experience that made you (even a little bit) famous.

People Say . . .

. . . a big fish in a small pond . . . —Saying

In the future, everyone will be famous for fifteen minutes.
        —Andy Warhol, American artist and author

What do these sayings mean?

Do you know of similar sayings?

Vocabulary Review

1. I have no idea what bands are popular these days. I don't _____ music news at all.

2. When European actors go to the United States, they sometimes feel _____ because Americans don't know who they are.

3. I saw my favorite singer at a restaurant and asked him for his _____ . He wrote it on a napkin.

4. Sarah saw her favorite tennis player at the museum yesterday. At first, she didn't _____ him, because he looked different than he does on TV.

5. The _____ was very surprised by the ending of the movie. Everyone thought Robert would marry Nicole, but he married her sister.

Famous People

Activity 3

1. Brad Pitt
2. Queen Elizabeth II
3. Colin Powell
4. Jennifer Lopez
5. Tiger Woods
6. Britney Spears
7. Shaquille O'Neal
8. Lance Armstrong
9. Arnold Schwarzenegger
10. Yo-Yo Ma
11. Kofi Annan
12. J. K. Rowling
13. Julia Roberts
14. Venus Williams
15. Bill Gates

3

Going to the Store or Shopping over the Internet?

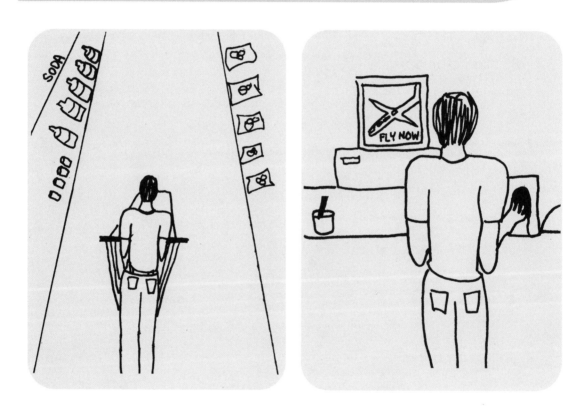

Starting Off

1. How often do you go shopping?

2. How often do you buy something over the Internet?

3. What is your favorite store?

4. Does your favorite store have a Web site? If so, have you visited it?

Vocabulary

navigate—(verb) find the way to or through a place

Most children can **navigate** their way through the Internet very easily.

Many explorers are famous because they were able to **navigate** the way to the New World.

customer—(noun) a person who pays for a service or item

Some store managers believe that the **customer** is always right.

If you have a problem at the store, you can always go to the **customer** service desk for help.

compare—(verb) look at two or more things to see how they are similar or different

Before you buy a new car, it is good to **compare** the different makes and models.

The Spanish girl always wanted to **compare** her English with that of a native speaker.

interaction—(noun) the activity of talking to other people, working with them, and so on

The **interaction** between a doctor and a patient should be positive.

The teacher had a lot of **interaction** with her students before and after class.

clerk—(noun) a person who works in a store and helps customers

The store was so big that it was hard to find a **clerk** to help us out.

When the **clerks** aren't helping customers, they keep the store organized.

Reading

In 2001, there were 47.6 billion sales over the Internet.* People have become more comfortable with the computer and can **navigate** around the Internet with ease. This may partially explain why the number of online sales is so high. Using a credit card over the Internet has become a safer experience now that information sent is encrypted. When information is encrypted, it's scrambled in such a way that makes it very secure. The average **customer** most likely visits a few sites before actually making a purchase. It is very easy to **compare** prices and find a good deal on shipping costs. If the trend continues, Internet sales are likely to go up.

▷ ▷ ▷ ▷ ▷ ▷ ▷

There are people who say they want nothing to do with this Internet shopping
t   t is important to these people to go to the store and touch the items they
            dering buying. Sometimes it is possible to test the item before buying it. If
            for example, you can smell it. If it's a CD player, you can play with the
            en you go to the store, the social experience includes **interactions**
            oppers and store **clerks.** Shopping malls are here to stay as far as
            s are concerned.

...ension Questions

1. In 2001, how many sales were made over the Internet?

2. What are two reasons that Internet sales have increased?

3. How many Internet sites does the average customer likely visit before making a purchase?

4. List three reasons why some shoppers like to go to the store to purchase items.

Discussion Activities

Activity 1

In a small group, discuss the advantages and disadvantages of Internet shopping and of going to the store. As you brainstorm your ideas, write them down in the chart that follows.

---

* Statistic from http://www.w3income.com/info.htm, accessed January 5, 2003.

Advantages of Internet Shopping	Disadvantages of Internet Shopping
Advantages of Shopping at a Store	Disadvantages of Shopping at a Store

Tommy and Sue want to buy a wedding gift for their friends who are getting married soon. They can't decide if they should go on the Internet to purchase a gift or if it would be better to visit the shopping mall. The class will form two groups and debate. Group A will try to convince the couple to go to the shopping mall to purchase the gift. Group B will try to convince the couple to use the Internet to buy the present. Before starting the debate, spend time in your groups talking about the advantages and disadvantages of both ways of shopping. Make sure everyone has a chance to participate in this discussion.

Conversation Tip

When you want to ask for more information, you can use these expressions:

Can you explain that?

What do you mean exactly?

A: There are so many advantages to shopping over the Internet.

B: **Can you explain that?**

A: Well, it can be cheaper, and you never have to leave your house.

Language Learning Tip

When you don't understand a word, you can use this expression:

What does _____ mean?

A: I think the Internet is easy to navigate.

B: Navigate? **What does that mean?**

A: It means "find your way to somewhere."

Try to use these tips in your discussion.

Wrap Up

Which group was more convincing?

What were the strengths and weaknesses of each group's presentation?

Activity 2

Is it better to shop over the Internet or go to a store? Look at the following list of items. Working individually, decide if it is better to shop over the Internet or go to the store for each item listed. You may decide that either method is fine. Be prepared to share your answers with the class.

Item	Internet	Store	Either	Why?
Camera	___	___	___	_____
Book	___	___	___	_____
CD player	___	___	___	_____
Plane ticket	___	___	___	_____
Shoes	___	___	___	_____
Wine glasses	___	___	___	_____
Dictionary	___	___	___	_____
Sweater	___	___	___	_____
Chocolate	___	___	___	_____
Paint brushes	___	___	___	_____

Which other items would you prefer to purchase over the Internet? Why?

1. _____

2. _____

3. _____

Which other items would you prefer to purchase at a store? Why?

1. _____

2. _____

3. _____

Work in small groups and compare your answers. Look back at the list of items. Did all the people in the group have similar answers? Be ready to share your answers with the class.

Activity 3

You were chosen to plan a small shopping mall near your house. You are responsible for deciding what stores will go into the shopping mall. Work with a partner. In the following charts, write the name of one store in each box. There will be 10 stores on the first level and 10 on the second level. When you are finished, share your final results with the class.

First Level of the Mall				

Second Level of the Mall				

What stores did you and your partner have an easy time agreeing on? Why?

What stores did you disagree on? Why?

How did you come up with a solution that you both agreed on?

Write about It

1. Describe a time that you had "buyer's remorse"—that is, when you regretted making a purchase. Explain.

2. What is one thing that you would like to buy? Why?

3. Do you prefer going to the store or buying something over the Internet? Explain.

People Say . . .

Sometimes the best purchase is the one you do not make. —Saying

The customer is always right. —Saying

What do these sayings mean?

Do you know of similar sayings?

Vocabulary Review

1. The _____ at the convenience store were busy helping other customers, so we had to wait our turn.

2. Before buying a big item, it is good to _____ prices to get the best deal around.

3. The food and service were so bad at the restaurant that one table of _____ got up and left without paying.

4. Once you've had some practice, it is easy to _____ your way around the Internet.

5. For a company to be successful, it's important that the _____ between the employer and employee be open and honest.

4

Friends or Acquaintances?

Starting Off

1. How did you meet most of your friends?

2. How often do you talk to your closest friends?

3. What do you talk about?

4. What do you and your friends do together?

Vocabulary

extremely—(adverb) very, really

The students couldn't pass the test, because it was **extremely** difficult.

I like this jacket, but it's **extremely** expensive. I don't have enough money to buy it.

lifetime—(noun) the time one is alive, the number of years one lives

My grandmother was always interested in learning. She studied many things during her **lifetime.**

Dr. James has spent a **lifetime** helping sick children all over the world.

acquaintance—(noun) someone you know, but who is not a close friend

I have an **acquaintance** in New York. I don't talk to him often, but sometimes we meet for lunch when I'm in New York.

An **acquaintance,** George, asked me if I would lend him some money. I only lend money to close friends or family members, so I said no.

otherwise—(adverb) if not, in another situation

Jessica goes to California once a year, but she doesn't travel **otherwise.**

I hope it snows tomorrow. **Otherwise,** we won't be able to ski.

fade—(verb) become weaker

This shirt was bright red when I bought it, but now the color is starting to **fade.**

Theresa and Harry have been married for 50 years, and their love has never **faded.**

Reading

For most Americans, friendships are **extremely** important, but there are different kinds of friendships. People who are "close friends" or "best friends" know just about everything about each other and trust each other completely. Such friends talk about everything: life, death, love, and dreams. If one friend has a problem, he or she will call the other, even if it's the middle of the night. They laugh together in happy times and cry together in sad times. Both know their friendship will last a **lifetime.**

▷ ▷ ▷ ▷ ▷ ▷ ▷

There are also friendships that are not so close. In the United States, this is common, in part because people move so often. People in these types of friendships may consider themselves to be **acquaintances** more than friends. They may only see each other or talk on the phone once in a while. They might discuss work, vacations, or family, but not more serious personal subjects. Many of these people might meet because they have common interests. For example, if two people both like to hike, they might occasionally go hiking together but **otherwise** rarely meet. If one of the people also likes tennis, he or she might have another friend who plays tennis, and those two might only meet occasionally to play tennis. These types of friendships may become stronger over time, or they may **fade** as people become busy with other interests.

Comprehension Questions

1. What do close friends talk about?

2. Why would one friend call another in the middle of the night?

3. What do acquaintances talk about?

4. How can the relationship between two acquaintances change?

Discussion Activities

Activity 1

In a small group, discuss the advantages and disadvantages of having a few close friends (instead of having many acquaintances) and of having many acquaintances (instead of having a few close friends). Write your answers in the chart that follows.

Advantages of Having a Few Close Friends	Disadvantages of Having a Few Close Friends
Advantages of Having Many Acquaintances	Disadvantages of Having Many Acquaintances

Discuss this topic as a class. The class will then form two groups. Group A will try to convince the class that having only a few good friends is better than having many acquaintances. Group B will try to convince the class that the opposite is true. Make sure that everyone has a chance to speak.

Conversation Tip

When you want to give someone more information, you can use these expressions:

What I mean is . . .

For example, . . .

A: I don't think I could live without my good friends.

B: You couldn't live?

A: **What I mean is** my friends are very important in my life.

Language Learning Tip

When you see a word and you don't know how to say it, you can use this expression:

How do you pronounce _____ ?

A: **How do you pronounce** the second word in this sentence?

B: Oh. That's "acquaintance."

A: Thank you.

Try to use these tips in your discussion.

Wrap Up

Which group was more convincing?

What were the strengths and weaknesses of each group's presentation?

Activity 2

Part 1

When people meet for the first time—at a party, for example—there are certain things they might say to start a conversation. Someone might begin by asking, "Do you know many people here?" Or one person might make a comment about another's clothes or jewelry, for instance, "I like your earrings. Where did you get them?" People might make these kinds of comments even before they introduce themselves.

Once the conversation has begun, the people might start talking about other topics, such as the weather, work, or their hometowns. This is called "small talk." Making small talk is an easy way to keep a conversation going, because most people are comfortable discussing those topics.

When people want to end a conversation, there are certain things that they might say. For example, at a party, someone might say, "Excuse me. I'm going to get another drink."

After saying something to end the conversation, the person may add, "It was nice meeting you."

The other person may then use one of these expressions, too.

Can you think of any expressions that are similar to the ones described above? Write them in the chart that follows.

Starting a Conversation

Do you know many people here?

Making Small Talk

Where are you from?

Ending a Conversation

Excuse me. I'm going to get another drink.

Adding a Comment

It was nice meeting you.

Here is an example of a complete conversation between two people meeting for the first time.

Person A and Person B are at a party. Person B is wearing a T-shirt that says "Paris, France."

A: That's a nice shirt. Did you get it in Paris?

B: *Yeah. I went there last summer.*

A: That's great. I've always wanted to go there. My name's Alan, by the way.

B: *I'm Brooke. Nice to meet you.*

A: So, how did you like Paris, anyway?

B: *Oh, it was beautiful, but the weather wasn't very good. It rained a lot.*

A: That's too bad. The same thing happened to me on my last vacation. I went to Florida, and it rained the whole time.

B: *Wow. I guess you didn't do much swimming.*

A: No. But I went to Disney World. That was fun. Have you been there?

B: *Not since I was a kid. I'd like to go again, though.*

A: Me, too, but not when it's raining. You know, I've got to find my friend Cal. I need to ask him something before he leaves.

B: *OK. It was nice meeting you.*

A: Nice meeting you, too.

Part 2
Pretend your classmates are all at a party, but you don't know each other. Everyone should stand up and find a partner. One person should begin the conversation. Then the two should talk about some of the topics described as small talk in part 1 of this activity (weather, work, hometowns) or about other, similar topics. When the teacher tells you to finish the conversation, one person should say something to show that the conversation is over.

Activity 3

Work with a partner. Think of a problem that two friends have. Write a dialogue in which the friends discuss the problem and try to solve it. Then act out the dialogue for your classmates.

Write about It

1. Describe why one of your friends is important to you.

2. Do you have a friend you have known for a very long time? Write about how your friendship has changed over the years.

3. What qualities do you look for in a friend? Do you look for the same qualities in an acquaintance?

People Say . . .

Friends are like stars. You don't always see them, but you know they're always there. —Saying

Friends are flowers in the garden of life. —Saying

What do these sayings mean?

Do you know of similar sayings?

4

Vocabulary Review

1. Most people get married once in their _____ , but some people never get married.

2. If the weather's nice, I'll go to the beach tomorrow. _____ , I'll stay at home.

3. When I was younger, I was _____ interested in art. I went to the museum every week. Now I don't care about art very much.

4. I've met Jennifer a few times, but I don't know her well. She's an _____ .

5. Peter was angry at Curt for a long time. Finally, Peter's anger _____ , and they became friends.

5

Summer **or** Winter?

Starting Off

1. Which do you prefer, summer or winter?

2. What are some activities that can only be done in the summer?

3. What are some activities that can only be done in the winter?

4. If you won a free vacation, would you choose a week in the Caribbean or a week skiing in the mountains? Why?

Vocabulary

relative—(noun) a member of your family

During the holidays, we spend a lot of time with **relatives.**

All of the **relatives** get together once a year for a family reunion.

escape—(verb) get away from place or a dangerous situation

The prisoner planned for years how to **escape** from the prison.

Many people want to **escape** the cold weather by going to a tropical island.

incredibly—(adverb) to a very great degree

The service at the new restaurant was **incredibly** slow.

It was **incredibly** cold outside, so the children had to stay in during recess.

temperature—(noun) the measure of how hot or cold a place or thing is

When mixing ingredients for baking a cake, the eggs should be at room **temperature.**

She felt sick, so the nurse took her **temperature.**

envision—(verb) imagine something, especially as a future possibility

He is **envisioning** the day when he gets married.

The parents **envisioned** their child being accepted to a great university.

Reading

In the Northern Hemisphere, summer begins around June 21. This day, which happens to be the longest day of the year, is known as the summer solstice. Summer is associated with beaches, bathing suits, and barbecue parties. Students daydream about long summer vacations during which they can visit **relatives** or go to overnight camp for a few weeks. When the weather is warm, people can enjoy outdoor activities such as swimming, sailing, and sunbathing. Even in places where there are likely to be some **incredibly** hot days, thoughts of summer can make people smile.

▷ ▷ ▷ ▷ ▷ ▷ ▷

The winter solstice falls on or around December 21 in the Northern Hemisphere. Instead of being the longest day of the year, it is the shortest, on which it is likely that the sun will set before 5:00 P.M. Even though winter days are shorter and the

temperature is colder, winter sports enthusiasts look forward to such activities as skiing and snowboarding. These people spend the warmer months **envisioning** the first snow of the upcoming winter season.

Comprehension Questions

1. When does the summer solstice occur in the Northern Hemisphere?

2. How do students spend their free time during the summer?

3. When is the shortest day of the year in the Northern Hemisphere?

4. List two winter activities mentioned in the reading.

Discussion Activities

Activity 1

In a small group, discuss the advantages and disadvantages of summer and of winter. Write your ideas in the chart that follows.

Advantages of Summer	Disadvantages of Summer
Advantages of Winter	Disadvantages of Winter

Chikako has been offered two jobs. Both jobs offer the same salary and have similar benefits. One job is located in Miami, Florida. The other job is located in Boulder, Colorado. Some of her friends think she should live in a place where there are no cold winter months. Her other friends think she should live somewhere where she can enjoy the four seasons. The class will form two groups and debate. Group A will try to convince Chikako to take the job in sunny Miami. Group B will try to convince her to take the job in snowy Boulder. Make sure everyone has a chance to participate in the discussion.

Conversation Tip

When you want to disagree and add your own opinion, you can use these expressions:

I know what you're saying, but . . .

That may be true, but . . .

A: Winter is a great time of year because you can go snowboarding.

B: **I know what you're saying, but** I think sailing on a hot summer day is much more enjoyable.

Language Learning Tip

If you don't understand what people say because they speak too quickly, you can use this expression:

Could you speak more slowly?

A: I just bought tickets for a hockey game.

B: I'm sorry. I didn't understand. Could you speak more slowly?

A: I bought tickets for a hockey game.

Try to use these tips in your discussion.

Wrap Up

Which group was more convincing?

What were the strengths and weaknesses of each group's presentation?

Activity 2

The Summer Olympics and Winter Olympics are held every four years. They are not held during the same year, but they used to be. Now, they are held on an alternating two-year schedule. That means that if the Summer Olympics were held this year, the Winter Olympics would be held in two years. Throughout the history of the Olympics, some sporting events have been eliminated. Your task is to define what the events are. What are these sports? How are they played? Ask a native English speaker about the sports below. What are the rules? When during the year is each sport played? What special equipment is needed? Be prepared to discuss your answers with the class.

Cricket How it is played	Croquet How it is played
Golf How it is played	Lacrosse How it is played

Polo How it is played	Rugby How it is played

Tug-of-War How it is played	Water Skiing How it is played

Imagine that you are the head of the Olympic committee. You have to choose one sport to be reintroduced into the Olympics. Spend time talking in your groups. Decide which sport should be chosen. Be ready to explain your answer to the class. Make sure you have an advantage and a disadvantage for each sporting event.

Our group decided to reintroduce _____ into the Olympics.	We thought this would be a good choice because _____ _____ .

Activity 3

Look at the grid below. Each box has some information in it. Find someone in your class who answers "yes" to that information. Once someone answers "yes," you have to move on to a new person. If you finish early, try to find a second person to answer "yes" to the information. When someone answers "yes," put the person's initials in the box.

Find someone who . . .

Likes to ski	Went swimming last week	Saw snow last year	Has a birthday in April
_____	_____	_____	_____
Is scared to drive in snow	Has been snowboarding	Likes the Summer Olympics	Knows where the next Winter Olympics will be
_____	_____	_____	_____
Knows where the next Summer Olympics will be	Has been skiing	Has had a sunburn	Has visited a Caribbean island
_____	_____	_____	_____
Hates snow	Owns a snow shovel	Has a favorite winter holiday	Doesn't have air-conditioning in the car
_____	_____	_____	_____

What did you learn about your classmates? Be prepared to share with the whole class a few interesting facts you learned.

Write about It

1. What is your favorite season?

2. Do you think the seasons affect a person's mood? Explain.

3. What is the climate like in a country your family came from?

People Say . . .

Snowy winter. Plentiful harvest. —Saying (Vermont)

We have two seasons: winter and Fourth of July. —Saying (New England)

What do these sayings mean?

Do you know of similar sayings?

Vocabulary Review

1. The movie was _____ bad, so people walked out before it was finished.

2. When we were renovating our house, we stayed with _____ for five months.

3. After she moved to Hollywood, Takako _____ herself becoming an actress in the movies.

4. The only way to _____ the cold is to sit in front of the fireplace with a cup of hot chocolate.

5. The _____ was below freezing for three weeks in a row, so the pond froze.

6

Type A **or** Type B?

Starting Off

1. Do you prefer to be busy, or do you prefer to relax?

2. Are you usually patient, or are you usually impatient?

3. Do you think there is a connection between one's answers to Questions 1 and 2 and one's health?

4. Do you think there is a connection between one's answers to Questions 1 and 2 and one's success at work?

Vocabulary

strive—(verb) try very hard to do something difficult

I'm **striving** to improve my English this year.

We'll **strive** to get to the top of the mountain, but we may not be able to.

obstacle—(noun) something that prevents you from moving forward or accomplishing a goal

There was an **obstacle** in the road, so David had to stop the car.

Not having computer skills can be an **obstacle** when one is looking for a job.

laid-back—(adjective) relaxed, not worried

My boss is very **laid-back.** She doesn't care what time I come to work.

Matilda is very nervous about getting married next week, but Jack is very **laid-back** about it.

hostile—(adjective) aggressive, easily angered

My neighbor is very **hostile.** He's always yelling at somebody.

Bears can be **hostile.** Sometimes they attack people.

link—(noun) connection, relation

There's a **link** between the amount of food one eats and one's weight. If you eat a lot, you'll gain weight.

There's no **link** between eye color and English ability. Some people with blue eyes speak English very well. Other people with blue eyes can't speak English at all.

Reading

Have you ever heard the terms *Type A* and *Type B* used to describe someone's personality? Two doctors in California, Meyer Friedman and Ray Rosenman, were the first to use these categories. They began researching the connection between personality and heart disease in the late 1950s. According to Friedman and Rosenman, people with Type A personalities are similar to each other in several ways.* For example, people with Type A personalities tend to be competitive.

---

*Barry L. Zaret et al., eds. *Yale University School of Medicine Heart Book* (New York: Hearst Books, 1992), 99–101.

These people always seem to be **striving** to reach some goal and often feel that some **obstacle** is in their way. Type As are especially concerned with time and always seem to be in a hurry. Type Bs are more **laid-back.** They are less competitive and more patient than Type As. Men and women who have the same personality type share many characteristics. Type A women, however, are usually less **hostile** than Type A men, according to Friedman and Rosenman.

▷ ▷ ▷ ▷ ▷ ▷ ▷

In their research, Friedman and Rosenman found a **link** between personality type and heart disease. More recently, other researchers have seen the same link. People who are competitive and always hurrying may succeed at work, but they may be damaging their health. For these people, relaxation may be as important as medicine.

Comprehension Questions

1. What are some ways to describe Type A personalities?

2. What are some ways to describe Type B personalities?

3. Does the reading describe any differences between Type A men and Type A women? If so, explain what the differences are.

4. Does the reading describe any differences between Type B men and Type B women? If so, explain what the differences are.

Discussion Activities

Activity 1

Friedman and Rosenman found that Type As and Type Bs differ from each other in their attitudes toward many things, including work. Which type of person do you think would be a better manager? In a small group, discuss the advantages and disadvantages of having a Type A person and of having a Type B person as a manager. Write your answers in the chart that follows.

Advantages of Having a Type A Manager	Disadvantages of Having a Type A Manager
Advantages of Having a Type B Manager	Disadvantages of Having a Type B Manager

The president of Funco Toys needs to hire a store manager for the company's new store in London. There are two excellent candidates: Gretchen, a Type A person; and Courtney, a Type B person. Both of the candidates have successfully managed other toy stores, but their styles of management are very different. Gretchen thinks that people work best when they are under pressure and feel a sense of competition. Courtney feels that people work best in a relaxed environment. The class will form two groups and debate. Group A will try to convince the president to hire Gretchen. Group B will try to convince the president to hire Courtney. During the discussion, make sure that everyone has a chance to speak.

Conversation Tip

When you want to show that you agree with someone, you can use these expressions:

Exactly.

That's for sure.

A: Ambroise is so laid-back. He must be Type B.

B: **That's for sure.** He never gets upset about anything.

Language Learning Tip

When you aren't sure how to spell a word, you can use this expression:

Could you spell that for me?

A: If you want to learn more about Type A and Type B, you should read Dr. Rosenman's research.

B: Rosenman? **Could you spell that for me?**

A: Sure. It's spelled R-O-S-E-N-M-A-N.

Try to use these tips in your discussion.

Wrap Up

Which group was more convincing?

What were the strengths and weaknesses of each group's presentation?

Activity 2

Work with a partner. Imagine that you have two friends, Oscar and Kyle, who are coming from out of town to visit you. Oscar and Kyle want to spend time with both of you and with each other. Oscar will arrive Friday night and leave Saturday night. He is basically a Type A person. Kyle will arrive Saturday and leave Sunday night. He is basically a Type B person. Decide on at least five activities for each day that you and your partner will do with your friends. Write your answers in the chart below.

Activities with Oscar on Friday	
Activities with Oscar and Kyle on Saturday	
Activities with Kyle on Sunday	

Discuss your answers with the class. What are some of the best ideas that your classmates had?

Activity 3

With a partner, perform a role play for the class. You are a patient, and your partner is a doctor. Tell your doctor about your lifestyle and personality. Your doctor will try to determine whether you are at risk for a heart attack and will give you advice on how to take care of your health.

Write about It

1. If you wanted to relax for a day, what would you do?

2. What would you like to change about your personality?

3. Do you think people are born with a certain personality, or do you think their personality is formed by their experiences?

People Say . . .

Patience doesn't always help, but impatience never does. —Russian saying

We take no delight in existence except when we are struggling for something. —Arthur Schopenhauer, German philosopher

What do these sayings mean?

Do you know of similar sayings?

Vocabulary Review

1. I wonder if eating certain foods can make a person smarter. Do you think there's any _____ between food and intelligence?

2. Becky's always smiling. She's never been _____ toward me.

3. Dennis works for a German company, but he can't speak German. That might be an _____ for him if he tries to get a more important job in the company.

4. Every day, he _____ to learn the language, but he thinks it's very difficult. I hope he doesn't give up.

5. Janice doesn't worry about anything. She's the most _____ person I know.

7

Having a Big Wedding or Eloping?

Starting Off

1. How many weddings have you attended?

2. Have you ever been to an unusual wedding? Explain.

3. How long does it take to plan a wedding?

4. How important is it to have a big reception after the wedding ceremony?

51

Vocabulary

average—(adjective) not unusually big or small

The **average** grade on the exam was 72 percent.

She works an **average** of 45 hours per week.

reception—(noun) a large formal party to celebrate an event or to welcome someone

The wedding **reception** was expensive because of the live band and the delicious dinner.

There was a **reception** for the famous author at the hotel, to promote his new book.

elope—(verb) go away secretly with someone to get married

If you want a quick wedding, you could **elope** and go to Las Vegas.

The teenagers didn't want to wait for a wedding, so they chose to **elope.**

exotic—(adjective) unusual and exciting because of a connection with a foreign country

Some people enjoy traveling to **exotic** places.

The San Diego Zoo has many **exotic** animals.

accommodations—(noun) a room in a hotel or other place where you stay while on vacation

The **accommodations** at a hotel are usually smaller than one is used to.

The hotel **accommodations** were so bad that the tourists complained and then changed hotels.

Reading

Some people spend years envisioning what their wedding day is going to be like. An **average** wedding costs about $20,000.* There is also a year or more of planning that includes finding a church, organizing a **reception,** and buying a

---

*Information from the On-Line Massachussetts Wedding Guide, at http://www.maweddingguide.com/planning/costs/costs.htm, accessed February 13, 2003.

wedding gown. Planning for a wedding involves not only the bride and groom but their parents, bridesmaids, and the best man. Having a big wedding may be expensive, but some people think it's worth it, because it's such a special occasion.

▶ ▶ ▶ ▶ ▶ ▶ ▶

When people consider how much it costs to have a big wedding, some decide that **eloping** is a much better option. A couple can get on a plane, fly to an **exotic** destination, and tie the knot for about $5,000.* Some vacation resorts offer a wedding travel package that includes the marriage ceremony, photographs, flowers, and **accommodations.** The money saved by not having a fancy wedding can help the couple buy a house. In addition to saving money, eloping is fun and unconventional. It might be a good story to tell the grandchildren.

Comprehension Questions

1. How much does a wedding cost on average?

2. Who is involved in the planning of a big wedding?

3. How much does it cost to elope?

4. What are some reasons people choose to elope over having a big wedding?

Discussion Activities

Activity 1

In a small group, discuss the advantages and disadvantages of having a big wedding and of eloping. Your opinions are important even if you have never been married. Write your answers in the chart that follows.

---

*Information from http://weddings.about.com/cs/budgeting/index.htm, accessed February 13, 2003.

Advantages of Having a Big Wedding	Disadvantages of Having a Big Wedding
Advantages of Eloping	**Disadvantages of Eloping**

Trisha and Ricardo have been engaged for two years. They want to elope to save money for a down payment on a house. Their parents are upset and think they should have a traditional wedding. The class will form two groups and debate. Group A will try to convince Trisha and Ricardo to give up their plans and have a big wedding instead. Group B thinks Trisha and Ricardo are smart to elope. This group will try to convince them to stick with their original plan to elope. During this discussion, make sure that *everyone* has a chance to speak.

Conversation Tip

When you want to show that you disagree with someone, you can use these expressions:

That's not what I think.

That's not the way I see it.

A: I think it's crazy to spend so much money on a wedding. It's only one day.

B: **That's not the way I see it.** I think it's the most important day in a person's life.

Language Learning Tip

When you don't understand what someone said, you can use this expression:

Could you repeat that?

A: Instead of having a big wedding, my partner and I are going to elope.

B: **Could you repeat that?**

A: We're getting married secretly.

Try to use these tips in your discussion.

Wrap Up

Which group was more convincing?

What were the strengths and weaknesses of each group's presentation?

Activity 2

A happy medium between having a big wedding and eloping is having a "destination wedding," where the bride and groom invite family members and everyone travels to another city to have the wedding. The cost is cheaper than that of a huge wedding.

Work with a partner. Imagine that you are each planning to get married and to have a destination wedding. Decide what each wedding will be like. Where will it take place? Who will be invited? How long will the trip take? Be prepared to share your answers with the class when you are finished.

Destination Wedding	Me	My Partner
Who will you invite?	_____	_____
	_____	_____
Where will it be?	_____	_____
How much do you want to spend?	_____	_____
How many days will it last?	_____	_____
What will you do with the money you save?	_____	_____

Activity 3

When planning a traditional wedding, many things need to be considered. In your opinion, what is necessary and what is not that important when thinking about getting married? Working alone, review the list and check off what you think is important and not that important for a wedding. When you are finished, compare your answers with a partner.

What	Necessary	Not That Important
Booking a church	____	____
Giving an engagement ring	____	____
Rehearsal dinner	____	____
Reception after ceremony	____	____
Wedding cake	____	____

What	Necessary	Not That Important
Flowers at ceremony	____	____
Flowers at reception	____	____
Having music	____	____
Photographer	____	____
Videographer	____	____
Bridesmaids	____	____
Best man	____	____
Gifts for guests	____	____
Exotic honeymoon	____	____
_____	____	____

What did you and your partner agree on?

What did you and your partner disagree on?

If there is time, talk about a wedding that you attended. Tell your partner about it.

Write about It

1. Describe a typical wedding, based on those you have attended.

2. What would be the reaction of family and friends if you or someone you knew eloped?

3. Describe your perfect wedding.

People Say . . .

Who marries for money earns it. —Saying

Marry your like. —Saying

What do these sayings mean?

Do you know of similar sayings?

Vocabulary Review

1. The visiting students have to pay for their own meals and _____ during the semester abroad.

2. The boy dreamed of traveling to _____ destinations, such as Fiji and Tahiti.

3. Planning a wedding was too overwhelming, so the couple decided to _____ to Aruba.

4. When the prime minister of Japan came to the university, there was a beautiful _____ held in his honor.

5. The _____ yearly rainfall on the island is about 25 inches.

Big City or Small Town?

Starting Off

1. What is your idea of the perfect place to live?

2. Why do some people prefer to live in big cities?

3. Why do some people prefer to live in small towns?

4. What are some differences between people in cities and people in small towns?

Vocabulary

ideal—(adjective) perfect

Matt's job is interesting, and the salary is good. The job is **ideal.**

Joanne says that Mark is the **ideal** man for her. She loves everything about him.

picture—(verb) imagine, *see in one's mind*

When I feel nervous, I **picture** a beautiful beach. Then I feel more relaxed.

I know I've met Frank, but I can't **picture** his face. I only remember his name.

urban—(adjective) related to cities

Urban life is exciting, but I like living in a small town because it's quieter.

Many people want to live in **urban** areas, so houses in cities are usually expensive.

rural—(adjective) related to small towns

I grew up in a very **rural** part of the country. There were a lot of farms, but not many people.

I love cities. I don't want to live in a **rural** place. I think it would be too boring.

bound—(adjective) expected (*is bound to* = will definitely)

I didn't study at all for the test. I'm **bound** to fail it.

If you exercise more and eat less, you're **bound** to lose weight.

Reading

When you think of the **ideal** place to live, do you **picture** a big city or a small town? Both can be great, but for very different reasons. In an **urban** area, there are always a lot of things happening. You can find all kinds of different restaurants, movies, art, and music. Cities are also likely to have the most job opportunities. In addition, cities often have good public transportation, which is very convenient for people who don't have cars.

▷ ▷ ▷ ▷ ▷ ▷ ▷

Rural areas have other advantages. For one thing, the pace of life is often slower in a small town, so people may feel more relaxed. People in a small town may also get to know each other well, because they see the same faces every day. Lastly, rural areas may offer beautiful scenery that can't be found in cities. Whatever your image of the perfect place is, there is **bound** to be a city or town somewhere that fits that description.

Comprehension Questions

1. What are some examples of entertainment available in a big city?

2. Why is it easy to travel in an urban area?

3. Why might people in small towns feel less stress than people in big cities?

4. Why do people in rural areas know each other better than people in urban areas?

Discussion Activities

Activity 1

Do you know which ten cities in the United States have the largest populations? Talk with a partner and try to guess. Write your answers below. Then discuss your answers with the class. (The real answers appear at the end of this chapter, but don't look at them until you have finished.)

1. _____   6. _____

2. _____   7. _____

3. _____   8. _____

4. _____   9. _____

5. _____   10. _____

In a small group, discuss the advantages and disadvantages of big cities and small towns. Write your answers in the chart that follows.

Advantages of Big Cities	Disadvantages of Big Cities
Advantages of Small Towns	Disadvantages of Small Towns

Anya wants to study abroad in an English language program, but she doesn't know whether she should study in a big city or a small town. The class will form two groups and debate. Group A will try to convince Anya to study in a big city. Group B will try to convince her to study in a small town. During the discussion, make sure that *everyone* has a chance to speak.

Conversation Tip

When you want to ask for more information, you can use these expressions:

Could you give me an example?

Could you be more specific?

A: I think a small town is the best place to learn English.

B: **Could you be more specific?**

A: In my opinion, people in small towns are friendlier and more talkative, so you get more of a chance to speak English.

Language Learning Tip

When you don't understand a word, you can use this expression:

What's the definition of _____ ?

A: According to this newspaper article, people in urban areas have more stress.

B: **What's the definition of "urban"?**

A: It means "related to cities."

Try to use these tips in your discussion.

Wrap Up

Which group was more convincing?

What were the strengths and weaknesses of each group's presentation?

Activity 3

Work in a small group. Imagine that you and the members of your group work for a travel agency and are going to make a TV commercial about a city or town somewhere in the world. Choose one place that will be the subject of your commercial, and discuss the best reasons to visit that place. After your discussion, write a script for the commercial, then practice it with your group. Finally, perform your commercial for the class, or make a video of it to show your classmates.

Write about It

1. Describe the best or worst points about your hometown.

2. How well do people in your town know each other? Explain with examples.

3. In your country, what is a town or city that many people want to live in? Why do people want to live there?

People Say . . .

A city is a large community where people are lonely together. —Saying

You can take the boy out of the country, but you can't take the country out of the boy. —Saying

What do these sayings mean?

Do you know of similar sayings?

Vocabulary Review

1. Linda left the house early, and there's not much traffic today, so she's

   _____ to get to work on time.

2. You don't see many trees in _____ areas, but you do see a lot of

   buildings.

3. I think spring is the _____ season. It's not too hot or cold, and the

   flowers are blooming everywhere.

4. My grandfather grew up in a very _____ place. There were only 20

   children in his school.

5. When I _____ my best friend, I imagine that she is smiling.

Activity 1
Largest U.S. Cities (population in the year 2000)

1. New York, New York (8,008,278)

2. Los Angeles, California (3,694,820)

3. Chicago, Illinois (2,896,016)

4. Houston, Texas (1,953,631)

5. Philadelphia, Pennsylvania (1,517,550)

6. Phoenix, Arizona (1,321,045)

7. San Diego, California (1,223,400)

8. Dallas, Texas (1,188,580)

9. San Antonio, Texas (1,144,646)

10. Detroit, Michigan (951,270)

———————

Source: Bureau of the Census, U.S. Department of Commerce, quoted in William A. McGervan, editorial director, *The World Almanac and Book of Facts, 2003* (New York: World Almanac Books, 2003), 403.

Video at Home **or** Movie at the Theater?

Starting Off

1. How often do you go to the movies?

2. How often do you rent videos or DVDs?

3. When was the last time you went to the movies?

4. What kind of movies do you like to see?

Vocabulary

trailer—(noun) an advertisement for a new movie that shows clips from it

> The people were upset when no **trailers** were shown before the feature presentation.

> It is common for movie studios to show **trailers** to small groups before they are released nationally.

huge—(adjective) very big

> Some of the new movie theater complexes are **huge.** There may be up to 20 theaters in one building.

> When children are asked to think of a **huge** animal, an elephant comes to mind.

generate—(verb) produce or make something

> The movie *Titanic* ended up **generating** about $1.8 billion.

> The high number of car sales **generated** profit for the company.

impressive—(adjective) admirable because of being very good, large, important, and so on

> The new art gallery showed some **impressive** work by new artists.

> The sunset last night was **impressive** because of all the colors in the sky.

suit—(verb) be acceptable or convenient for a particular person

> Exercising in the morning **suits** her best.

> He has been so happy at his new job, so it must **suit** him.

Reading

Many people are movie buffs and will see a movie the day it opens. In 2001, Americans spent $8.4 billion on movie ticket sales alone.* Going to the movies is more than just seeing a movie. The moviegoer gets out of the house and sees **trailers** for upcoming movies. Many theaters boast high-quality sound, stadium

---

*Statistics from http://www.mpaa.org/useconomicreview/2001Economic/sld001.htm, accessed February 10, 2003.

seating, and **huge** screens. In addition, concession stands at theaters provide convenient snacks, including popcorn, candy, ice cream, and fast-food items.

▶ ▶ ▶ ▶ ▶ ▶ ▶

There are many people who wait for a movie to come out on video or DVD. In 2001, video and DVD rentals in America **generated** an **impressive** $21.5 billion.* Also, 96 percent of American households have at least one VCR, so a lot of people watch videos at home. Staying home to view a movie is much less expensive than going to the movies. It's also more convenient, because you can control the movie and view it when it **suits** your schedule.

Comprehension Questions

1. How much money did Americans spend on movie tickets in 2001?

2. What are some reasons people give for going to the movies?

3. What percentage of American households owns a VCR?

4. How much money did people spend on renting videos and DVDs in 2001?

Discussion Activities

Activity 1

In a small group, discuss the advantages and disadvantages of going to the theater and of staying home to watch a movie. Fill in the chart that follows.

---

*Statistics from http://www.business2.com/articles/mag/0,1640,39362,FF.html, accessed February 24, 2003.

Advantages of Going to the Movies	Disadvantages of Going to the Movies

Advantages of Renting a Video/DVD	Disadvantages of Renting a Video/DVD

It has been a long week for Tracy. She has plans to spend time with a few of her friends on Friday night. She can't decide if she should invite her friends over to watch a video or if she and her friends should go to the movie theater to see a movie. The class will form two groups and debate. Group A will try to convince Tracy to invite all of her friends over to watch a video. Group B will try to convince Tracy to go to the movie theater with her friends. Make sure everyone has a chance to participate in the discussion.

Conversation Tip

When you want to give someone more information, you can use these expressions:

In other words, . . .

What I'm trying to say is . . .

A: Renting videos is much better than going to the movies.

B: You don't like going to the movies?

A: No, I like going to the movies. **What I'm trying to say is** that I like renting videos even more.

Language Learning Tip

When you see a word and you don't know how to say it, you can use this expression:

How do you say _____ ?

A: Oh, look. There's a Japanese movie playing at the theater downtown. **How do you say** the director's name?

B: I think you say "Kurosawa."

Try to use these tips in your discussion.

Wrap Up

Which group was more convincing?

What were the strengths and weaknesses of each group's presentation?

Activity 2

Look at the following situations. In each case, decide which would be better, going to the movies or renting a video.

Be prepared to explain your answers.

Situation

Bob and Sally have just started
dating. This is their third date.   Go to the movies _____   Rent a video _____

Situation

John and Tina are married and
have two children (ages 3 and 6).   Go to the movies _____   Rent a video _____

Situation

Patrick and Darla are married and
have three children (ages 12, 14,
and 16).   Go to the movies _____   Rent a video _____

Situation

Tom is a single man who lives in
New York City.   Go to the movies _____   Rent a video _____

Situation

Tamara is a single woman who lives
in the suburbs (outside of the city).   Go to the movies _____   Rent a video _____

Situation

Arnold and Patricia are a
retired couple.   Go to the movies _____   Rent a video _____

Situation

Five high school friends want to
get together.   Go to the movies _____   Rent a video _____

Situation

A small group of college students
want to get together.   Go to the movies _____   Rent a video _____

Activity 3

Work in a small group. Imagine you are a group of movie directors and producers planning to make a new movie. You need to come up with the story, the location, and the actors. Write out your plan in the lines that follow. When you are done planning, you will "pitch" your plan to the whole class. After hearing all of the plans, the class will decide which movie plan to choose.

Your Plan

Story: (Give a summary of the story.) _____

_____

_____

_____

Location: (Where will you film this movie? Explain why you chose this location.)

_____

_____

_____

_____

Actors: (Who will star in the movie?) _____

_____

_____

_____

Write about It

1. What is your favorite movie? Why?

2. Who is your favorite movie star? Why?

3. Is it better to go to the movies alone or with other people? Explain.

People Say . . .

It's the only business where you can sit out front and applaud yourself.
—Will Rogers, American actor and humorist

You're only as good as your last picture.
—Marie Dressler, Canadian-American actress

What do these sayings mean?

Do you know of similar sayings?

Vocabulary Review

1. Building a new factory in the town was expected to _____ more than three hundred jobs in the community.

2. At the hockey game, they went to the concession stand and spent ten dollars on a hot dog, an order of onion rings, and a large soda. They were surprised that the portions were so _____ .

3. The college students watched some _____ on TV that advertised the upcoming holiday movies.

4. After studying English for a year, she received an _____ score on the TOEFL exam.

5. Ideally, a person should find a job that _____ his or her personality.

10

Time **or** Money?

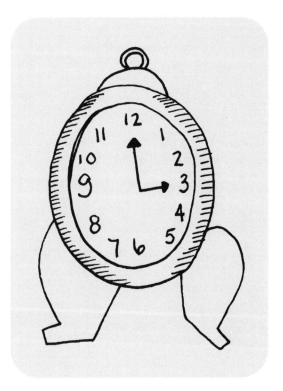

Starting Off

1. Why do people work?

2. How many hours a day do you work or study?

3. What do you do in your free time?

4. Do you think people have more or less free time in some countries than in others?

Vocabulary

obvious—(adjective) easy to see, easy to know

> Rose always gets good grades. It is **obvious** that she studies a lot.

> Exercising is an **obvious** way to lose weight.

labor—(noun) physical work

> I painted my house myself. I had to buy the paint, but I didn't have to pay anyone for the **labor.**

> My grandfather worked hard all his life. Because of his **labor,** he was able to buy a house.

industrialized—(adjective) developed, advanced, with many factories

> Japan has become very **industrialized** in the last 50 years.

> When I was a child, there were more farms in my state. Now it's very **industrialized.**

roughly—(adverb) about, nearly

> I sleep **roughly** eight hours a night. Sometimes I sleep more, and sometimes I sleep less.

> She looks older than I am, but we're **roughly** the same age.

off—(adjective) free, without work

> I have two jobs now, so I don't have much time **off.**

> In the United States, most teachers have the month of July **off.**

Reading

People work for many reasons, but the most **obvious** one is probably money. People have to pay their bills, and they need money to buy food and clothes. Of course, they also want to have money to eat out, go to the movies, and go on vacation. People work hard all year to earn enough money, but do they have enough time to enjoy it? In the United States, the answer may be no.

▷ ▷ ▷ ▷ ▷ ▷ ▷

According to the United Nations' International **Labor** Organization,* Americans work more than anyone else in the **industrialized** world. Australians, Canadians, Japanese, and Mexicans, for example, work about 100 hours fewer per year than Americans. That's about 2 and a half weeks fewer. People in Brazil and Great Britain work about 5 weeks fewer than Americans, and Germans work **roughly** 12 and a half weeks fewer. Would most Americans like more time **off?** Sure. That question is easy. Would they be willing to work less in exchange for less money? That's a little more difficult. How would you answer?

Comprehension Questions

1. Name some of the industrialized countries referred to in the reading.

2. Who works more per year, people from Canada or people from Great Britain?

3. How much time off do Germans have compared to Japanese?

4. Do Americans like working as much as they do?

Discussion Activities

Activity 1

In a small group, discuss the advantages and disadvantages of having more time off but earning less money. Then discuss the advantages and disadvantages of getting paid more but having less time off. Write your answers in the chart that follows.

---

*Information from Porter Anderson, "Study: U.S. Employees Put in Most Hours." *CNN.com,* August 31, 2001, available at http://www.cnn.com/2001/career/trends/08/30/ilo.study, accessed March 4, 2002.

Advantages of Having More Time Off but Less Money	Disadvantages of Having More Time Off but Less Money
Advantages of Having More Money but Less Time Off	**Disadvantages of Having More Money but Less Time Off**

Wayne works for a computer company and makes an average salary. He is 30 years old and single. Recently, Wayne was talking to his boss and mentioned that he's always busy. Wayne's boss said that she would be willing to reduce the amount of hours he works if he would accept a lower salary. Wayne could work four days a week instead of five, but his salary would be cut by 20 percent. Wayne would still work about the same number of hours each day as he does now. The class will form two groups and debate. Group A will try to convince Wayne to accept the boss's offer. Group B will try to convince Wayne to continue working five days a week. During the discussion, make sure that everyone has a chance to speak.

Conversation Tip

When you want to disagree and add your own opinion, you can use these expressions:

I see what you mean, but . . .

That's a good point, but . . .

A: I want to get another job because then I can make extra money.

B: **I see what you mean, but** then you won't be able to spend as much time with your family.

Language Learning Tip

If you don't understand what people say because they speak too quickly, you can use this expression:

Would you mind saying that again more slowly?

A: I'm so excited. I'm going on vacation next week.

B: **Would you mind saying that again more slowly?**

A: I'm excited about going on vacation.

Try to use these tips in your discussion.

Wrap Up

Which group was more convincing?

What were the strengths and weaknesses of each group's presentation?

Activity 2

Work in a small group. Imagine that the members of your group work at the same company and want more time off but no reduction in salary. Discuss the best way to make this argument to the company's management. Then write a letter explaining your proposal.

Give your letter to another group. They will act as the management and discuss why they should accept or reject your proposal. Then they will write a letter back to you.

Activity 3

In the chart that follows are the names of 10 countries in alphabetical order. Try to put them in order according to average hourly work compensation for production workers. Compensation includes the money one earns as well as other benefits, such as health insurance. The highest and lowest amounts are already given. Try to guess the remaining amounts of compensation. After you finish, look at the answers that appear at the end of this chapter.

Alphabetical Order	In Order of Compensation (highest to lowest)	Amount of Compensation (in U.S. dollars per hour)
1. Canada	1.	1. $22.86
2. France	2.	2.
3. Germany	3.	3.
4. Italy	4.	4.
5. Japan	5.	5.
6. Mexico	6.	6.
7. South Korea	7.	7.
8. Taiwan	8.	8.
9. United Kingdom	9.	9.
10. United States	10.	10. $2.34

Write about It

1. What would you do if you had more money?

2. What would you do if you had more free time?

3. What would be the perfect schedule for you?

People say . . .

Time is money. —Saying

Money can't buy happiness. —Saying

What do these sayings mean?

Do you know of similar sayings?

Vocabulary Review

1. I'm a little taller than my brother, but we're _____ the same height.

2. I have to work every day this week. I don't have any time _____ .

3. That car is really dirty. It's _____ that no one has washed it for a long time.

4. Gary stopped working at noon, so he only got paid for three hours of _____ .

5. Many people in _____ countries have computers in their homes.

Activity 3
Hourly Average Compensation for Production Workers in the Manufacturing
Industry, 2001

1. Germany $22.86

2. United States $20.32

3. Japan $19.59

4. United Kingdom $16.14

5. France $15.88

6. Canada $15.64

7. Italy $13.76

8. South Korea $8.09

9. Taiwan $5.70

10. Mexico $2.34

Source: Bureau of Labor Statistics, U.S. Department of Labor, quoted in William A. McGervan, editorial director, *The World Almanac and Book of Facts, 2003* (New York: World Almanac Books, 2003), 147.

11

Bagels or Doughnuts?

Starting Off

1. What do you usually eat for breakfast?

2. What did you eat for breakfast when you were younger?

3. What is your definition of a "healthy" breakfast?

4. What is your definition of an "unhealthy" breakfast?

Vocabulary

legend —(noun) an old well-known story

Many cultures have their own **legends** about how the earth started.

There is a **legend** about animals living on the moon.

honor—(verb) treat with special respect

The students wanted to **honor** their teacher after she had been at the school for 25 years.

Citizens around the world **honored** those who died in the war.

emigrate—(verb) leave one's country to live permanently in another country

Many people who live in the city **emigrated** from many different countries.

The family finally **emigrated** to the United States after thinking about it for a long time.

tradition—(noun) a belief, custom, or way of doing something that has existed for a long time

One American **tradition** is to eat turkey on Thanksgiving.

We have a family **tradition** of exchanging gifts on Christmas Eve.

version—(noun) a copy of something that is slightly different from other forms of it

There was more than one **version** of the story available on the Internet.

Across the country, there are many **versions** of recipes for apple pie.

Reading

Did you know that the bagel is the only bread product that is boiled before it is baked? According to **legend,** in the 1600s, bagels were given to women in Poland who were giving birth. There's another story about a baker from Vienna who wanted to **honor** King Jan Sobreski from Poland for saving the city from Turkish invaders. In 1683, he baked bread in the shape of a stirrup, after which the popularity of the bagel began. *Bagel* is the Austrian word for "stirrup." Many people who **emigrated** from various European countries to the United States brought the bagel **tradition** with them. Now people eat bagels for breakfast, for lunch, or as a snack.

▶▶▶▶▶▶▶

Doughnuts (whose name is also spelled "donuts") have been around for a long time. A doughnut is a piece of dough that has been fried in oil. Many countries have their own **versions** of this combination. The Dutch are credited with taking sweet balls of dough and cooking them in oil. These cakes were called *olykoeks,* or "oily cakes." In the 1600s, when the Pilgrims went to Holland before sailing to North America, they brought this recipe with them. The story is that the middle of the *olykoek* was removed so that the cake would cook all of the way through when it was fried. Now, not only are doughnuts available, but the doughnut holes can also be purchased.

Comprehension Questions

1. Who were bagels first given to in the 1600s?

2. Why did a Viennese baker want to honor King Jan Sobreski?

3. In which country did *olykoeks* originate?

4. How did the doughnut recipe make its way to North America?

Discussion Activities

Activity 1

In a group, discuss the advantages and disadvantages of bagels and doughnuts. Write your answers in the chart that follows.

Advantages of Bagels	Disadvantages of Bagels

Advantages of Doughnuts	Disadvantages of Doughnuts

Mustafa has offered to get the food for a breakfast meeting that is going to be held at his office. He needs to bring enough food for 15 people. He can't decide if he should bring bagels or doughnuts. The class will form two groups and debate. Group A will try to convince Mustafa to bring bagels to the meeting. Group B will try to convince him to bring doughnuts. Make sure that everyone has a chance to participate in the discussion.

Conversation Tip

When you want to show that you agree with someone, you can use these expressions:

I agree.

That's right.

A: I think chocolate doughnuts are the best.

B: **I agree.** They're my favorite.

Language Learning Tip

When you aren't sure how to spell a word, you can use this expression:

How do you spell that?

A: Could you get me a French cruller at the Donut Shack?

B: Cruller? **How do you spell that?**

A: You spell it C-R-U-L-L-E-R.

Try to use these tips in your discussion.

Wrap Up

Which group was more convincing?

What were the strengths and weaknesses of each group's presentation?

A c t i v i t y 2

Think about how your breakfast habits have changed over the years. You may eat breakfast at a different time than you once did. You may consume different food now compared to some point in the past. Work with a partner to fill in the chart that follows.

Time Frame	Your Breakfast Habits	Partner's Breakfast Habits
Childhood		
Teenage years		
After high school		
Now		

When you have finished the chart, discuss the following questions with your partner.

1. Have your breakfast choices changed as you have gotten older? If so, how? Why?

2. Do you think your breakfast choices will change in the future? If so, how? Why?

Circulate around the classroom. Find classmates who answer "yes" to the following questions. Once a person answers "yes," write down his or her initials and move on to a new person. If you finish early, try to find additional people to answer "yes" to your questions. Pay attention to the question word when asking a question.

Find someone who . . .

Rarely eats breakfast	Ate a donut yesterday	Eats a bagel at least once a week
_____	_____	_____
Wants to eat eggs tomorrow	Always eats breakfast at home	Often eats breakfast at a coffee shop
_____	_____	_____
Doesn't like bagels	Doesn't like donuts	Is hungry right now
_____	_____	_____

Write about It

1. Describe a typical breakfast.

2. Write about your favorite breakfast foods.

3. Imagine that you were living 200 years ago. Describe what you would have eaten for breakfast.

People Say . . .

All happiness depends on a leisurely breakfast.
—John Gunther, American journalist

Eat breakfast like a king, lunch like a prince, and dinner like a pauper.
—Adelle Davis, American nutrionist and author

What do these sayings mean?

Do you know of similar sayings?

Vocabulary Review

1. Many people _____ from Europe to South America during World War II.

2. The university wanted to _____ the dean who was retiring at the end of the year.

3. There is a _____ about Johnny Appleseed, the man who people say was responsible for planting apple trees in America.

4. Although there are many _____ of the computer program available, they wanted the newest one.

5. Most football teams have a _____ of pouring a bucket of water over the coach if they win a championship game.

Left-Brain Person or Right-Brain Person?

Starting Off

1. What different learning styles do students have?

2. How do you best learn new information?

3. Are people born with certain skills, or do they learn them?

4. Are you a more logical person or an intuitive person? Explain.

Vocabulary

hemisphere—(noun) one of the two hemispheres of your brain, one of the halves of the earth

Cutting an orange in half would make it look like a **hemisphere.**

People live in either the Northern **Hemisphere** or the Southern **Hemisphere.**

logical—(adjective) reasonable

It is not **logical** to study for an exam after you take it.

There must be a **logical** explanation for what he did.

imagination—(noun) the ability to form pictures and ideas in your mind

The child, who had a wonderful **imagination,** wrote a story about talking animals.

Reading helps develop the **imagination.**

holistic—(adjective) reflecting the idea that a person or a thing needs to be treated as a whole

Doctors are taking a more **holistic** approach when they see patients.

Some teachers only use test scores to grade a student. Other teachers use a more **holistic** approach and look at things such as grades, participation, and homework.

dominant—(adjective) stronger and more important than other people or things

In genetics, brown eyes are **dominant,** and blue eyes are recessive.

Many people had a hard time dealing with her, because of her **dominant** personality.

12

Reading

There are two **hemispheres** in the brain that control how and what we do. The *left brain* controls right-hand movement, spoken and written language, number skills, and scientific language. Left-brain individuals tend to think in a **logical,** linear manner. These people speak somewhat slowly. Schools tend to stress logical-analytical thinking, which makes them centered on left-brain tasks.

▷▷▷▷▷▷▷

The *right brain* controls left-hand movement, **imagination,** spatial relations, and music and art awareness. Right-brain individuals tend to think in a nonsequential, **holistic** way. These people often speak very quickly. It is possible for people to exercise both sides of the brain so that neither side is **dominant.** Einstein, who was a terrific scientist (left brain), was also an accomplished violinist (right brain).

Comprehension Questions

1. How many hemispheres are there in the brain?

2. List four things that the left hemisphere of the brain controls.

3. List four things that the right hemisphere of the brain controls.

4. What musical instrument did Einstein play?

Discussion Activities

Activity 1

Part 1

In a small group, discuss the advantages and disadvantages of being a left-brain person and of being a right-brain person. In the chart that follows, write down as many ideas as you can think of for each topic. You may want to take the left-brain/right-brain quiz in part 2 before starting the discussion.

Advantages of Being a Right-Brain Person	Disadvantages of Being a Right-Brain Person
The advantages that she can increas her sense tives and she will be a good creative maybe she will be genius!	she will discencess control silfish, practical

Advantages of Being a Left-Brain Person	Disadvantages of Being a Left-Brain Person

Polly and Greg are married and have a five-year-old boy, Joshua. They are ready to enroll him in school. There are two schools that offer a terrific education. The Edison School is a "left-brain" school, which focuses on analytical, linear thinking. There is an emphasis on science and math. The Bellview School, on the other hand, is a "right-brain" school, which focuses on nonsequential thinking. There is an emphasis on art and music. Both schools have sent their graduates to wonderful colleges and universities. The class will form two groups and debate. Group A will try to convince Polly and Greg to enroll Joshua in the Edison School. Group B will try to convince Polly and Greg to enroll Joshua in the Bellview School. Make sure everyone participates in the conversation.

Wrap Up

Which group was more convincing?

What were the strengths and weaknesses of each group's presentation?

Conversation Tip

When you want to show that you disagree with someone, you can use these expressions:

I disagree.

I don't think so.

A: I think you might be a left-brain person, because you're so good with spoken language.

B: **I don't think so.** I have a really hard time speaking English.

Language Learning Tip

When you don't understand what someone has said, you can use this expression:

Could you say that again?

A: You seem like a right-brain person to me, because you see things in a nonsequential way.

B: **Could you say that again?**

A: You know, you don't always have to keep things in a certain order.

Try to use these tips in your discussion.

H. J

Activity 1

Part 2

Read the following sets of statements. In each set, circle the answer that best describes you. Do this individually.

1. a. I am better at recognizing names.

   b. I am better at recognizing faces.

2. a. I take time to make decisions.

   b. I make decisions very quickly.

3. a. I like to read realistic stories.

   b. I like to read stories based on fantasy.

4. a. I use facts to solve a problem.

   b. I solve a problem using intuition.

5. a. I like tasks that have a clear beginning and end.

   b. I like tasks where I can decide what to do when.

6. a. I remember things best using words.

   b. I remember things best using pictures.

7. a. I am not very creative. I like to stick with what I know.

   b. I am always very creative and have many new ideas.

8. a. Many of my thoughts are serious.

   b. I have many humorous, funny ideas.

9. a. When I read, I read for details.

   b. When I read, I read for the main idea.

10. a. I learn best by using lists and plans.

   b. I learn best by freely exploring a topic.

11. a. I like competitive sports.

    b. I like non-competitive sports.

12. a. My work-space is usually neat.

    b. My work-space is usually messy.

13. a. I rarely lose track of time.

    b. I often lose track of time.

14. a. I am logical and good with numbers.

    b. I am imaginative and creative.

Count how many *as* and *bs* you circled, and write your total numbers here.

Total *as*: __6__   Total *bs*: __8__

If you circled mostly *as*, you're dominated by the left brain, which makes you a scientist! You're probably better at numbers and objective data than with creative tasks. You would do well in a career involving mathematics, business, science, engineering, etc.

If you circled mostly *bs*, you're dominated by your right brain, which makes you an artist! You are probably highly creative. You would do well in a creative field, such as graphic arts, writing, music, photography, etc.

If you circled an *even* number of *as* and *bs*, that means that you do not have a dominant hemisphere.

Activity 2

Choose three people in the class. In the following spaces, write each person's name and indicate whether you think the person is left-brain or right-brain dominant. To find out if your predictions are correct, ask each student whether he or she agrees. Record your classmates' answers.

Name	Left- or Right-Brain Dominant? (my guess)	Left- or Right-Brain Dominant? (classmate's answer)
1. _____	_____	_____
2. _____	_____	_____
3. _____	_____	_____

When you are finished, share your results with the class.

Were you surprised at any of your classmates' answers?

Activity 3

Work with a partner or in a small group. Look at the following list of professions. Discuss which professions are more likely to be left-brain dominant and which are more likely to be right-brain dominant. For each profession, write down your decision and explain how you made it.

Profession	Left- or Right-Brain Dominant?	Why?
Airplane pilot	_____	_____
Computer programmer	_____	_____
Artist	_____	_____
Medical doctor	_____	_____
Interpreter	_____	_____
Athlete	_____	_____
Movie director	_____	_____
Screenplay writer	_____	_____
Teacher	_____	_____
Chef	_____	_____

Profession	Left- or Right-Brain Dominant?	Why?
Stockbroker	_____	_____
Nurse	_____	_____
Graphic artist	_____	_____
Journalist	_____	_____

Add three more professions to the list.

_____	_____	_____
_____	_____	_____
_____	_____	_____

Write about It

1. Describe your favorite teacher of all time.

2. Are you a right-brain learner or a left-brain learner? Explain.

3. Describe a time that you had to work very hard at learning something. What did you learn? How did you go about it?

People Say . . .

We learn only from those whom we love. —Goethe, German poet

Learn one thing well first. —John Clarke, physician and minister

What do these sayings mean?

Do you know of similar sayings?

Vocabulary Review

1. Many people believe that children need to be exposed to a _____ approach to education.

2. If you have a vivid _____ , it may be easier for you to write a science fiction story.

3. Because of her strong personality, she was the _____ one on the team.

4. To be successful at computer programming, it is necessary to think in a _____ way.

5. One _____ of the brain is stronger, but both are being used all the time.

13

Working for a Company or Being Self-Employed?

Starting Off

1. Is anyone in your family self-employed?

2. If you work for someone else, do you have greater security?

3. Does it take a special personality to be self-employed? Explain.

4. Which would you prefer, working for a company or being self-employed?

Vocabulary

allow—(verb) let something happen

The teacher **allows** her students to miss two classes each semester.

The employers **allow** the staff to take their pets to work.

benefits—(noun) money or advantages from a job

Sara quit her job because there were very few **benefits.**

There are many **benefits** for those who choose to stay in school.

complain—(verb) say that you are unhappy about someone or something

All of the students **complained** when the teacher announced there would be a test in two days.

The employees **complained** when they heard there would be no raises this year.

worry—(verb) be anxious or unhappy about something

Parents usually **worry** when their children are driving at night.

Todd always **worries** that he won't do well in his classes, even though he studies three hours a night.

salary—(noun) the amount of money one makes from working

Peter decided to become a plastic surgeon in Hollywood because of the high **salary.**

Kelly put half of her weekly **salary** in the bank because she was saving for a new car.

Reading

Being self-employed may look easy from the outside, but it involves a lot of hard work. Self-employment **allows** you, the business owner, to set your own hours. There is also the chance of earning much more than those who work for others. Starting up a business lets you do business your own way, as there is no boss to answer to. Once you are successful as a business owner, you can enjoy all the **benefits** that come with working for yourself.

▷▷▷▷▷▷▷

Many people **complain** about having to work for someone else, even though it is not as bad as they say. Unlike for a business owner, your hours are usually set. If you end up working more hours than agreed upon, you will probably be compensated. This may be in the form of extra pay or an additional day off. Because the company **worries** about all the financial risks, you don't have to worry about bankruptcy. Having a steady paycheck is a comfort for many. In addition to the **salary,** many employees receive benefits, which may include health insurance and a retirement plan.

Comprehension Questions

1. What kind of hours does someone who is self-employed usually work?

2. Does a business owner always make more than someone who works for a company?

3. What may happen if someone in a company works more hours than usual?

4. What are some possible benefits a company worker may receive?

Discussion Activities

Activity 1

In a small group, discuss the advantages and disadvantages of working for a company and of being self-employed. Write your answers in the chart that follows.

Advantages of Being Self-employed	Disadvantages of Being Self-employed
Advantages of Working for Someone Else	Disadvantages of Working for Someone Else

Barbara is graduating from business school in six months. She is very eager to start her own coffee shop. Some friends tell her to start her own business, so she can be her own boss. Others think she should manage a coffee shop that has already been established so that she can get some experience.

The class will form two groups and debate. Group A will try to convince Barbara that she shouldn't lose any time working for someone else. She should take a risk and start her own business. Group B will try to convince Barbara that she needs more experience. There is a lot of risk involved. Barbara will also have a lot of school loans to repay, so she needs to make a certain amount of money each month. Make sure everyone has a chance to participate in the conversation.

Conversation Tip

When you want to ask for more information, you can use these expressions:

Can you explain that?

What do you mean exactly?

A: Starting up your own business can be very risky.

B: **What do you mean exactly?**

A: Well, if the business fails, you might lose a lot of money.

Language Learning Tip

When you don't understand a word, you can use this expression:

What does _____ mean?

A: Jim's new job is great. He's got a high salary.

B: **What does "salary" mean?**

A: It means "the amount of money you make."

Try to use these tips in your discussion.

Wrap Up

Which group was more convincing?

What were the strengths and weaknesses of each group's presentation?

Activity 2

Is self-employment for you? Take the quiz that follows. Answer each question yes or no. First, answer the questions independently. Then, get in a group and discuss your answers.

	Yes	No
1. Do you always follow through on a project?	____	____
2. Are you a positive person?	____	____
3. Are you good at solving problems?	____	____
4. Do you enjoy taking risks?	____	____
5. Do you get along with almost everyone?	____	____
6. Do you work hard?	____	____
7. Are you an organized person?	____	____
8. Do you enjoy freedom?	____	____
9. Are you flexible?	____	____
10. Are you responsible?	____	____
11. Are you good at selling things?	____	____
12. Are you energetic?	____	____
13. Do you have a lot of self-confidence?	____	____
14. Are you healthy?	____	____

Count how many questions you answered yes, and write your number here: _____

If you have 0–5 yes answers, you should work for someone else.

If you have 6–10 yes answers, you may be nervous at first, but starting a business could work for you.

If you have 11–14 yes answers, you could be ready to start your business today.

In a group, compare your results with those of your classmates and discuss the following questions.

1. Do you enjoy working for others? Why or why not?

2. Do you think you have what it takes to start your own business? Why or why not?

Share your answers with the whole class.

Activity 3

You are going to work in pairs or small groups. You were given $100,000 and now you and your business partner(s) are going to start a business. Think about a business that you haven't seen but think would be successful.

What kind of business will it be? _____

Where will it be located? _____

Why do you think this business will be successful? _____

_____

What kind of people do you think your business will attract? _____

_____

When you are finished planning your business, share your business ideas with the whole class.

Write about It

1. Describe your dream job.

2. Describe the process of getting a job.

3. Is it popular for teenagers to have part-time jobs? Explain.

People Say . . .

Nothing is really work unless you would rather be doing something else.
—James M. Barrie, Scottish journalist, playwright, and novelist

By working faithfully eight hours a day, you may eventually get to be a boss and work twelve hours a day. —Robert Frost, American poet

What do these sayings mean?

Do you know of similar sayings?

Vocabulary Review

1. The new pitcher for the baseball team was making the highest _____ on the team.

2. In the middle of winter, people often _____ about the cold weather.

3. The employer thought it was important to offer her employees good _____ , which included medical and dental insurance.

4. The mother sometimes _____ her children to stay up late if they finish all of their homework assignments.

5. Bob's girlfriend always _____ when he doesn't call after he arrives home safely from a long business trip.

14

Fiction or Nonfiction?

Starting Off

1. Why do people read books?

2. What kinds of books do you like?

3. Describe a book that was very entertaining to you.

4. Describe a book that taught you a lot.

Vocabulary

fiction—(noun) something that is not true, an untrue story

I only read books about real events. I never read **fiction.**

I'm taking a class in **fiction** writing this year. Everyone in the class has to write a story.

momentarily—(adverb) for a short time

The bird sat on the roof **momentarily** and then flew away.

When the baby dropped his toy, he cried **momentarily,** but soon he began to smile again.

flexibility—(noun) room for freedom

There is some **flexibility** in the schedule. We can start any time between 8:00 A.M. and 10:00 A.M.

The teacher said that we have to write exactly three pages. We don't have any **flexibility.**

encompass— (verb) include

The United States **encompasses** land from the Atlantic coast of North America to the Pacific coast.

Zach is a very active man. His interests **encompass** all kinds of sports and outdoor activities.

obscure—(adjective) little known, hard to understand

My professor wrote a book about the history of western Massachusetts between 1850 and 1865. It's a very **obscure** topic. I don't think many people bought the book.

Barry likes some very **obscure** singers. I've never heard of any of them.

Reading

When authors write **fiction,** they can create worlds in their own minds and make those worlds come alive on the pages of a book. Because their writing doesn't have to be real, they are free to make up the most interesting stories they can. Some fiction authors write about international spies, space travel, or romance. These stories may be a way for readers to escape their everyday lives and experience a world of excitement, at least **momentarily.**

▶▶▶▶▶▶▶

Compared to fiction writers, authors of nonfiction don't have as much **flexibility** when writing a book, because all of the details in a nonfiction book must be true. Nonfiction authors do, however, write about a wide variety of subjects. Nonfiction **encompasses** history, biography, politics, science, and many other areas. People often choose to read nonfiction because they want to learn more about a particular subject. Even if you're interested in something **obscure,** someone has probably written a book about it. Naturally, most people don't read only fiction or nonfiction. They read both. Yet they may read different types of books for different reasons. Whether you want to study or just relax, a book can help you do it.

Comprehension Questions

1. Why might fiction be more interesting than nonfiction?

2. Why might someone want to read fiction?

3. What are four categories of nonfiction?

4. Why might someone want to read nonfiction instead of fiction?

Discussion Activities

Activity 1

In a small group, discuss the advantages and disadvantages of fiction and of nonfiction. Write your answers in the chart that follows.

Advantages of Fiction	Disadvantages of Fiction
Advantages of Nonfiction	Advantages of Nonfiction

Your class has decided to read a book and discuss it. The problem is that you can't decide on what type of book to read. The class will form two groups and debate. Group A will try to convince the class that it should read a work of fiction. Group B will try to convince the class that a work of nonfiction would be better. During this discussion, make sure that everyone has a chance to speak.

Conversation Tip

When you want to give someone more information, you can use these expressions:

What I mean is . . .

For example, . . .

A: I like cookbooks. They always teach me new things.

B: What do you learn from cookbooks?

A: A lot. **For example,** I learn how to make new dishes, and I learn what food is popular in other countries.

Language Learning Tip

When you see a word and you don't know how to say it, you can use this expression:

How do you pronounce _____ ?

A: I saw this word in a cookbook. **How do you pronounce** it?

B: You pronounce it "kim chee." It's a kind of Korean food.

A: Oh. I've heard of that.

Try to use these tips in your discussion.

Wrap Up

Which group was more convincing?

What were the strengths and weaknesses of each group's presentation?

Activity 2

Sometimes authors may mix fact and fiction. For example, they may write about an experience they had or a person they know, but they may change a few of the details. Of course, this can make some people very upset. In a small group, discuss the following situations.

Imagine that your friend wrote a story about some secret you told him or her. Even if your friend didn't use your real name in the story, people might know the story was about you. How would you feel?

Imagine that you are a writer and your friend has told you about an embarrassing incident from his or her life. You told your friend that it would make a great story, but your friend wants you to promise never to write about it, even if you change some of the facts. You think that the story could make you a successful author. Will you promise not to write about it?

Activity 3

In this activity, you and a partner will write a story, and the other pairs in the class will guess whether the story is fiction or nonfiction. Begin by telling your partner about a funny, interesting, or surprising incident in your life. Pick an incident that the other pairs in the class don't know about. If possible, try to choose something that your classmates might not believe. Next, your partner should tell you about an incident from his or her life. You and your partner should then write a story together about one of three things: the incident you described, the incident your partner described, or something fictional. If you choose to write fiction, try to make it somewhat believable. After the writing is finished, the pairs should read their stories to the class. After a pair reads its story, the other pairs must guess whether the story is fiction or nonfiction. If a pair guesses correctly, it gets a point. The pair with the most points at the end of the readings wins.

Write about It

1. Describe a book that you would like to write one day.

2. Who is your favorite character from a book? Why do you like that person?

3. What are some things we can't learn from books?

14 _____

People Say . . .

Truth is stranger than fiction. —Saying

The good end happily, and the bad unhappily. That is what fiction means.
—*Oscar Wilde,* Irish dramatist, poet, and novelist

What do these sayings mean?

Do you know of similar sayings?

Vocabulary Review

1. We've learned many things about English. Our class _____ reading,

writing, grammar, and pronunciation.

2. My parents used to live in Los Angeles. Now they live in a tiny,

_____ town. You can't even find it on a map.

3. Monique only reads the newspaper and books about art. She never reads

_____ .

4. My friend and I are planning a vacation together. I have to leave on a Friday,

but he has some _____ . He can leave on any day of the week.

5. The phone rang _____ , and then the ringing stopped. Someone

must have answered it.

15

Diet or Exercise?

Starting Off

1. Have you ever been on a diet?

2. How often do you exercise?

3. In your opinion, how long do people successfully stay on diets?

4. How does the media influence the way we diet and exercise?

Vocabulary

ethical—(adjective) morally good or bad

That may be legal, but is it **ethical?**

It is not **ethical** for doctors to operate on members of their family.

committed—(adjective) willing to work hard at something

People in the neighborhood are **committed** to building a new playground.

She is **committed** to her job, so she works long hours.

sedentary—(adjective) not moving or exercising very much

America's young people spend too much time on the computer, so they are **sedentary.**

People with **sedentary** lifestyles have a higher risk of heart disease.

diabetes—(noun) a disease in which there is too much sugar in the blood

Diabetes is becoming a common disease because people eat more junk food.

Diabetes is sometimes hereditary.

obesity—(noun) the condition of being too fat in a way that risks good health

There are many health risks related to **obesity,** including heart disease and high cholesterol.

Obesity is increasing among children, because they are exercising less than they should.

Reading

People diet for a variety of reasons. At any given time, about 65 million Americans are on a diet. People may choose to diet due to health concerns, issues with weight or appearance, or **ethical** or religious reasons. Some people are devoted to total vegetarianism and avoid all animal products. Some are **committed** to low-carbohydrate diets where they try to avoid such foods as pasta, bread, and sweets. Others adhere to portion control but eat without dietary restrictions. There are many diets available to suit the needs of many individuals.

▷▷▷▷▷▷▷

Some people maintain a healthy weight through exercise, rarely focusing on dietary habits. Sixty percent of American adults don't get the required exercise needed for good health.* Adults live a **sedentary** life, so it takes a special effort to incorporate cardiovascular exercise, strength training, and flexibility stretching into their daily routines. Those who do exercise decrease their risk of such health problems as heart disease, **diabetes,** and **obesity.** Once people start to exercise on a regular basis, they feel so good that they usually stick with it.

Comprehension Questions

1. How many Americans are on a diet at any given time?

2. List three reasons why people go on a diet.

3. What percentage of American adults doesn't exercise?

4. What are some benefits of regular exercise?

Discussion Activities

Activity 1

In a small group, spend time talking about diet and exercise. Brainstorm the advantages and disadvantages of dieting and of exercising. Write your answers in the chart that follows.

*Statistic from http://www.healthclubs.com/benefits/body5.html, accessed December 20, 2002.

Advantages of Dieting	Disadvantages of Dieting
Advantages of Exercising	**Disadvantages of Exercising**

Martha wants to lose 20 pounds for her vacation to Hawaii, which will start six weeks from now. She thinks that if she loses 20 pounds, she will look and feel better when wearing a bathing suit. The class will form two groups and debate. Group A will try to convince Martha that she should go on a diet to lose the weight. Group B will try to convince Martha that she should start up an exercise routine to lose the weight.

Conversation Tip

When you want to disagree and add your own opinion, you can use these expressions:

> **I know what you're saying, but . . .**

> **That may be true, but . . .**

A: Kenji lost a lot of weight by only eating grapefruit.

B: **That may be true, but** it's very unhealthy to only eat one kind of food.

Language Learning Tip

If you don't understand what people say because they speak too quickly, you can use this expression:

> **Could you speak more slowly?**

Try to use these tips in your discussion.

Wrap Up

Which group was more convincing?

What were the strengths and weaknesses of each group's presentation?

Activity 2

List ten ways that you get exercise on a regular basis without really thinking about it. An example of this may be walking to the bus station.

1. _____

2. _____

3. _____

4. _____

5. _____

6. _____

7. _____

8. _____

9. _____

10. _____

List ten ways that each of your great-great-grandparents might have gotten exercise on a regular basis without thinking about it.

Great-great-grandfather   Great-great-grandmother

1. _____   1. _____

2. _____   2. _____

3. _____   3. _____

4. _____   4. _____

5. _____   5. _____

6. _____   6. _____

7. _____   7. _____

8. _____   8. _____

9. _____   9. _____

10. _____   10. _____

Discuss the following questions with your classmates.

1. What changes have occurred over the last 100 years regarding views on dieting and exercising?

2. What do you think diet and exercise habits will be like in 100 years? Will the changes be positive or negative?

Activity 3

List one advantage and one disadvantage of each of the following diet plans.

1. High carbohydrate (pasta, rice, bread, potatoes), low fat

   Advantage _____   Disadvantage _____

2. High protein (meat, fish, eggs, chicken), low carbohydrate

   Advantage _____   Disadvantage _____

3. Ovo-lacto vegetarian (no meat, but eggs and dairy are OK)

   Advantage _____   Disadvantage _____

4. Vegan (no animal products at all)

   Advantage _____   Disadvantage _____

5. Raw foods (no food heated over 114°F; mainly fruits and vegetables)

   Advantage _____   Disadvantage _____

6. No diet—accept whatever size you are

   Advantage _____   Disadvantage _____

Think about the goals Martha had from activity 1. Rank the diets in order from the best one for her to follow to the worst one for her to follow. Explain to the class how you decided to rank the diets.

1. _____ (best)

2. _____

3. _____

4. _____

5. _____

6. _____ (worst)

Write about It

1. What is a "fad diet"? Explain one fad diet that you have heard of or have tried.

2. What would be your ideal way to lose weight?

3. What is one healthy change you would like to make in your life?

People Say . . .

Whenever I feel the urge to exercise I lie down until it goes away.
—Anonymous

If you wish to grow thinner, diminish your dinner.
—Henry Sambrooke Leigh, English author and dramatist

What do these sayings mean?

Do you know of similar sayings?

Vocabulary Review

1. Because she has _____ , she has to give herself a shot of insulin every day.

2. Robert has a _____ job, so he makes sure that he exercises at least four times a week.

3. Barbara is _____ to getting a high score on the TOEFL exam, so she studies extra hard.

4. It is not _____ for politicians to get votes by giving people free gifts.

5. Some people think that the recent epidemic of _____ is partially caused from restaurants serving very big portions to its customers.

Early Bird **or** Night Owl?

Starting Off

1. What time do you usually wake up?

2. What time do you usually go to bed?

3. What are your favorite things to do in the morning?

4. What are your favorite things to do at night?

Vocabulary

accomplish—(verb) do something important, reach a goal

John F. Kennedy died when he was still young, but he **accomplished** many things in his short life.

I want to **accomplish** a lot during my summer vacation. I plan to read 20 books and learn how to play the violin.

drowsy—(adjective) tired, sleepy

I just took some medicine, and it made me **drowsy,** so I don't want to drive.

I felt so **drowsy** during the meeting that I almost fell asleep.

solitary—(adjective) alone, away from others

Martin lives a very **solitary** life. In fact, he rarely leaves his house.

Hardly anyone was at the beach. I just saw one **solitary** person walking toward the ocean.

determine—(verb) decide something, influence an outcome

The president of the company **determines** each employee's salary.

The amount of rain **determines** how well the flowers grow.

shift—(noun) required working time, usually eight hours

My **shift** doesn't end until 5:00 P.M., but I can meet you after that.

Beth works the late **shift,** so she doesn't get home until morning.

Reading

What did you do before 8:00 A.M. today? If your answer is, "I slept," you're definitely not an early bird. An early bird is someone who likes to wake up early and start his or her day while other people are still in bed. Some early birds get to their office before anyone else and start their work while the place is still quiet. Others go to the gym and exercise while the sun is coming up. Early birds can **accomplish** a lot before the sun sets. However, they start to feel **drowsy** when some people are just getting ready to start their evening.

▷▷▷▷▷▷▷

Night owls are people who regularly stay up late. Some night owls enjoy going to parties that last all night, or they might spend their time on more **solitary** activities, such as reading or studying. There are also people who stay up all night because their job **determines** what time they can go to bed. For example, they might work the night **shift,** from midnight to 8:00 A.M. Like early birds, night owls are awake when many of the people they know are sleeping. Although their schedules are very different, early birds and night owls still interact. In fact, a night owl who is coming home might run into an early bird who is leaving.

Comprehension Questions

1. What are two things an early bird might do in the morning?

2. What are two things a night owl might enjoy doing at night?

3. Why might some people stay up late even if they don't want to?

4. What is an example of an early bird and a night owl interacting?

Discussion Activities

Activity 1

In this activity, you and a partner will tell each other about your schedules. Listen to your partner describe his or her most recent day of school or work. Then, according to what he or she says, make a schedule like the example that follows. Write your partner's schedule in the space provided after the example. Switch roles. Then check with each other to see that you have written down everything correctly. Finally, talk about your schedules. Which one of you is more of an early bird? Which one is more of a night owl? What are the differences and similarities in your schedules?

Example Schedule

6:00 A.M.	sleep	6:00 P.M.	exercise at gym
7:00 A.M.	wake up/shower/breakfast	7:00 P.M.	
8:00 A.M.	drive to work	8:00 P.M.	drive home/dinner
9:00 A.M.	start work	9:00 P.M.	call friends
10:00 A.M.		10:00 P.M.	study English/write a letter
11:00 A.M.		11:00 P.M.	go to bed
12:00 P.M.		12:00 A.M.	
1:00 P.M.	lunch	1:00 A.M.	
2:00 P.M.		2:00 A.M.	
3:00 P.M.		3:00 A.M.	
4:00 P.M.		4:00 A.M.	
5:00 P.M.	finish work/drive to gym	5:00 A.M.	

_____ 's Schedule

6:00 A.M.	6:00 P.M.
7:00 A.M.	7:00 P.M.
8:00 A.M.	8:00 P.M.
9:00 A.M.	9:00 P.M.
10:00 A.M.	10:00 P.M.
11:00 A.M.	11:00 P.M.
12:00 P.M.	12:00 A.M.
1:00 P.M.	1:00 A.M.
2:00 P.M.	2:00 A.M.
3:00 P.M.	3:00 A.M.
4:00 P.M.	4:00 A.M.
5:00 P.M.	5:00 A.M.

Activity 2

In a small group, discuss the advantages and disadvantages of being an early bird and of being a night owl. Write your answers in the chart that follows.

Advantages of Being an Early Bird	Disadvantages of Being an Early Bird
Advantages of Being a Night Owl	**Disadvantages of Being a Night Owl**

Imagine that your school is considering changing its schedule. The new schedule will be either an "early bird" or a "night owl" schedule. The class will form two groups and debate. Each group should explain why its type of schedule is the best. During the discussion, make sure that everyone has a chance to speak.

Conversation Tip

When you want to show that you agree with someone, you can use these expressions:

> **Exactly.**

> **That's for sure.**

A: Getting up early on the weekends is wonderful because you can get so many things done.

B: **Exactly.** I'm up by seven every Saturday and Sunday.

Language Learning Tip

When you aren't sure how to spell a word, you can use this expression:

> **Could you spell that for me?**

A: I stayed up so late last night that I feel really drowsy right now.

B: Drowsy? I'm going to look that word up in the dictionary. **Could you spell that for me?**

A: You spell it D-R-O-W-S-Y.

Try to use these tips in your discussion.

Wrap Up

Which group was more convincing?

What were the strengths and weaknesses of each group's presentation?

Activity 3

Work with a partner. Cindy, Mitch, and Neil work in a convenience store that is open 24 hours a day. Each one of them works five eight-hour shifts per week. You and your partner are the store managers. Each of you works three eight-hour shifts per week. You and your partner must make up a three-week schedule for the store, keeping in mind that no one likes to work the "graveyard shift" (midnight to 8:00 A.M.) and that no one likes to work weekends. The shift from 8:00 A.M. to 4:00 P.M. is the most popular. How will you make a schedule that is fair? Will you give your employees the best shifts, or will you take them for yourselves? Write your schedule in the chart that follows. Then discuss it with the class, explaining your decisions.

Week 1

	Sun.	Mon.	Tues.	Wed.	Thurs.	Fri.	Sat.
12 A.M.–8 A.M.							
8 A.M.–4 P.M.							
4 P.M.–12 A.M.							

Week 2

	Sun.	Mon.	Tues.	Wed.	Thurs.	Fri.	Sat.
12 A.M.–8 A.M.							
8 A.M.–4 P.M.							
4 P.M.–12 A.M.							

Week 3

	Sun.	Mon.	Tues.	Wed.	Thurs.	Fri.	Sat.
12 A.M.— 8 A.M.							
8 A.M.– 4 P.M.							
4 P.M.– 12 A.M.							

Write about It

1. Do you think there are more early birds or more night owls? Why do you think so?

2. What is your favorite time of day (or night)? Why?

3. Imagine that you could only go outside at night. Describe a typical night in your life.

People say . . .

The early bird catches the worm. —Saying

Early to bed and early to rise, makes a man healthy, wealthy and wise.
—Benjamin Franklin, American philosopher and statesman

What do these sayings mean?

Do you know of similar sayings?

Vocabulary Review

1. Kim likes to be around other people. Her sister, however, is more

   _____ .

2. Ed works during the morning, and his girlfriend works at night. They don't see

   each other very much, because their _____ are so different.

3. If you start to feel _____ , I'll drive. I don't want you to drive if you're tired.

4. Your score on the final exam will _____ your grade for the course.

5. My brother quit high school and hasn't worked in a year. All he does is watch TV. My mother doesn't think he'll ever _____ anything.

Pack Rat
or Minimalist?

Starting Off

1. Do you enjoy collecting things? If so, what?

2. How often do you get rid of things that you own?

3. Are you an organized or a disorganized person?

4. Do you have a hard time throwing things out?

Vocabulary

sentimental—(adjective) based on feelings rather than practical reasons

She kept all of her old letters because they had **sentimental** value.

Losing the necklace her grandmother gave her made her sad, because she is very **sentimental.**

discard—(verb) get rid of something

My friend always **discards** old clothes when she buys new ones.

The old man hates to **discard** things, so his garage is filled with old newspapers and magazines.

outdated—(adjective) not useful or modern anymore

They tried to sell their old computer, but because it was **outdated,** nobody wanted to buy it.

Some of the information in the geography book was **outdated,** so the publisher printed a new edition.

acquire—(verb) get

The company recently **acquired** three new buildings.

Studying on our own allows us to **acquire** new knowledge.

clutter—(noun) a lot of things that are scattered in a messy way

The children usually end up with a lot of **clutter** on the floor after they play with their toys for the whole afternoon.

The president of the company tends to have a lot of **clutter** on her desk.

Reading

A pack rat is someone who enjoys holding onto various items from the past. Some pack rats are collectors who enjoy collecting particular items as a hobby, such as coins or stamps. Some pack rats hold onto old items because they think the items will be useful in the future. Pack rats may hold onto items for **sentimental** reasons even if the item is not useful. One thing is for sure, pack rats have a lot of stuff all around their homes.

▷ ▷ ▷ ▷ ▷ ▷ ▷

A minimalist is someone who enjoys empty space more than stuff. A minimalist **discards** items when they are **outdated** or have no current use. A minimalist is constantly following the "something in, something out" rule: that is, once you **acquire** something new, you must get rid of something old. Many minimalists claim that when **clutter** decreases, the peace and serenity around them increase. Some people have made a profession out of de-cluttering the homes and offices of pack rats!

Comprehension Questions

1. What is a pack rat?

2. What are three reasons pack rats like to hold on to their possessions?

3. What is a minimalist?

4. What is one rule a minimalist follows?

Discussion Activities

Activity 1

In a small group, discuss the advantages and disadvantages of being a pack rat and of being a minimalist. In the chart that follows, write down as many ideas as you can think of for each topic.

Advantages of Being a Pack Rat	Disadvantages of Being a Pack Rat
Advantages of Being a Minimalist	**Disadvantages of Being a Minimalist**

Daria and Marcelo are having a lively discussion about pack rats and minimalists. Daria thinks a pack rat should marry a pack rat and that a minimalist should marry a minimalist. There will be fewer arguments, according to Daria. Marcelo thinks opposites attract and that a pack rat would be happier married to a minimalist. The class will form two groups and debate. Group A will try to convince Marcelo that a pack rat should marry a pack rat, and that a minimalist should marry a minimalist. Group B will try to convince Daria that a pack rat should marry a minimalist. Make sure everyone participates in the conversation.

Conversation Tip

When you want to show that you disagree with someone, you can use these expressions:

> **That's not what I think.**

> **That's not the way I see it.**

A: I would get rid of grandma's wedding gown. No one's ever going to wear it.

B: **That's not what I think.** Old styles always come back into fashion.

Language Learning Tip

When you don't understand what someone said, you can use this expression:

> **Could you repeat that?**

A: My brother is such a minimalist. You should see his apartment.

B: **Could you repeat that?**

A: My brother's a minimalist. You know, he has almost nothing in his apartment.

Try to use these tips in your discussion.

Wrap Up

Which group was more convincing?

What were the strengths and weaknesses of each group's presentation?

Activity 2

Imagine you are moving to a studio apartment, in which space is very limited. You tend to be a pack rat and have accumulated many things over the years. Look at the list of items to get rid of.

First, work alone. Rank the items in the order of what you will get rid of first.

My Ranking	Item	Group Ranking
____	old textbooks	____
____	photos from elementary school	____
____	trophies and awards	____
____	old love letters	____
____	old clothes that no longer fit well	____
____	grandma's wedding gown	____
____	many issues of an old magazine	____
____	toys from childhood	____
____	an old sofa you want to fix up	____

Next, work in a small group and rank the above items again. Did your answers change at all?

Did your individual list differ from the group list? In what way?

Activity 3

In the spaces, list names of people you know. They could be family members, friends, or people you work with. Decide if each person you list is a pack rat or a minimalist. Give an example for each person. When you are finished, share your answers with your classmates.

Name: _____

Relationship: _____

Check one: pack rat ____   minimalist ____

Example: _____

Name: _____

Relationship: _____

Check one: pack rat ____   minimalist ____

Example: _____

Name: _____

Relationship: _____

Check one: pack rat ____   minimalist ____

Example: _____

Name: _____

Relationship: _____

Check one: pack rat ____   minimalist ____

Example: _____

Name: _____

Relationship: _____

Check one: pack rat ____   minimalist ____

Example: _____

Write about it

1. Imagine you had to move into a smaller space. What would you keep, and what would you get rid of?

2. Are you a pack rat or a minimalist? Explain.

3. Describe a time when you had to discard many of your things.

People Say . . .

There must be more to life than having everything.
—Maurice Sendak, American writer and illustrator

The best things in life aren't things. —Art Buchwald, American columnist

What do these sayings mean?

Do you know of similar sayings?

Vocabulary Review

1. Where did you _____ that new car?

2. The high school girls felt that their clothes were _____ , so they went to the mall to buy some new outfits.

3. Before the couple moved, they _____ all of the old things they no longer needed.

4. Even though it wasn't worth much, the old woman kept all of her old jewelry for _____ reasons.

5. Sam decided to get rid of all the _____ on his desk at work.

18

Love at First Sight or Love over Time?

Starting Off

1. Why do people fall in love?

2. Do men and women fall in love for the same reasons?

3. How do you know when you're in love?

4. How long does it take to fall in love?

Vocabulary

survey—(verb) ask many people the same set of questions to collect information

The car company **surveyed** 1,000 people about their favorite colors. Then the company produced cars in the five most popular colors.

After **surveying** the students, the cafeteria staff learned that most of them liked pizza.

skeptical—(adjective) not believing things easily

Leon was always **skeptical.** He didn't even believe in Santa Claus when he was a child.

My friend told me she quit smoking two weeks ago, but I'm **skeptical.** I think she's still smoking.

illusion—(noun) something that may seem real but actually is not

Bill and Wendy looked happy, but their happiness was an **illusion.** In fact, they both wanted a divorce.

When the Taylors went out of town, they left on some of the lights in their house to create the **illusion** that they were home.

compatible—(adjective) fitting together or matching well

This software will not work with my computer. The software and the computer are not **compatible.**

I am quiet and go to bed early. My roommate always stays up late and makes a lot of noise. I don't think we are **compatible.**

sensible—(adjective) using thought, not emotion

Tom is not very **sensible.** He always buys candy on his way to school. Then he doesn't have any money to buy lunch.

Andy wanted french fries, but he was **sensible** and ordered a salad because he was trying to lose weight.

Reading

Do you believe in love at first sight: that is, do you think it's possible to see a person for the first time and immediately fall in love with that person, before the two of you have even spoken? According to the 2000 Harlequin Romance Report,* 63 percent of the people who were **surveyed** (7,000 people in 22 countries) believe in it. In fact, 52 percent said they had experienced it. Of course, love at first sight has a lot to do with physical attraction. For example, a man may first be attracted to a woman because of her hair or eyes. However, love at first sight also involves a certain feeling that is difficult to describe: the feeling a person gets when he or she looks at someone and suddenly knows that the two of them belong together.

▶ ▶ ▶ ▶ ▶ ▶ ▶ ▶

Many **skeptical** people believe that love at first sight is only an **illusion.** They think that physical attraction can take place right away but that love takes much longer. Over time, two people can get to know each other and see whether they are **compatible.** Then the two might fall in love. People who believe in love over time may be **sensible,** but doesn't the idea of love at first sight seem romantic?

Comprehension Questions

1. What percentage of people do not believe in love at first sight?

2. How do you know when you have experienced love at first sight?

3. According to skeptical people, what is the difference between physical attraction and love?

4. How do people find out whether they are compatible?

---

*Statistics from http://www.everythingvalentine.com/bemyvalentine/harlequinsurvey.asp, accessed November 10, 2002.

18

Discussion Activities

Activity 1

The class will form two groups. Each group will discuss the reasons why love at first sight could be real and the reasons why it could be an illusion. Write your reasons in the boxes that follow. Try to think of reasons that weren't discussed in the reading.

Reasons Love at First Sight Could Be Real	Reasons Love at First Sight Could Be an Illusion

Your teacher will tell you a true or imaginary story about how he or she saw somebody and fell in love at first sight. (Some examples for the teacher appear at the end of this chapter.) Group A will try to convince the teacher that the experience was love at first sight. Group B will argue that it was an illusion. During the discussion, make sure everyone has a chance to speak.

Conversation Tip

When you want to ask for more information, you can use these expressions:

> **Could you give me an example?**
>
> **Could you be more specific?**

A: I think it was really love at first sight when they met.

B: **Could you be more specific?**

A: Well, she said she felt like she had known him all her life, but they had only just met. That has to be love at first sight.

Language Learning Tip

When you don't understand a word, you can use this expression:

> **What's the definition of _____ ?**

A: I don't think it was love at first sight. I think it was an illusion.

B: **What's the definition of "illusion"?**

A: Oh, an illusion is something that may seem real but actually is not.

Try to use these tips in your discussion.

Wrap Up

Which group was more convincing?

What were the strengths and weaknesses of each group's presentation?

Part 1

Interview your partner using the questionnaire.* Circle the letter for each of your partner's answers. The answers may show whether or not your partner believes in love at first sight.

1. Do you talk to people about your feelings?

    a. Yes, I talk to everyone about my feelings.

    b. I only talk to my close friends and family about my feelings.

    c. I keep my feelings to myself.

2. Have you ever experienced love at first sight?

    a. many times

    b. I thought so, but later I learned it wasn't really love.

    c. No.

3. Whose personal questions will you answer?

    a. my doctor's, my family's, and my best friend's

    b. my family's and my best friend's

    c. my best friend's

4. Where is the best place to find love?

    a. anywhere

    b. work or school

    c. bars and cafés

---

*Adapted from *Heart Clicks,* http://login.maxis.net.my/maxisnet/heartclicks/v3/quiz/love_first_sight.asp, accessed August 28, 2003.

5. You're alone in an elevator and someone you are attracted to gets in. What do you do?

   a. ask for a phone number

   b. smile at the person

   c. do nothing

6. Someone you are attracted to starts talking to you. What do you do?

   a. enjoy the conversation

   b. get very nervous but keep talking

   c. get too nervous to speak

7. What are your strong points?

   a. honest and reliable

   b. sincere and spontaneous

   c. modest

Calculate your partner's score.

For every *a* answer, give your partner 1 point.
For every *b* answer, give 2 points.
For every *c* answer, give 3 points.

```
Partner's score: _____
```

Check your and your partner's scores against the score key at the end of this chapter.

Do you think the survey is accurate? What questions would you add? Discuss these questions as a class.

Activity 3

Imagine that you see someone and think you have fallen in love at first sight. What would you say to that person to start a conversation? With a partner, try to come up with at least five ways to begin a conversation for each of the situations that follow.

Situation 1

You are a man waiting for a bus. You see a woman who is waiting for the same bus and feel your heart begin to pound. You are sure she is the woman for you. What will you say?

_____

_____

_____

_____

_____

Situation 2

You are a woman shopping at the grocery store. You see a man looking over the vegetables. Time seems to stop. You are sure he is the man of your dreams. What will you say?

_____

_____

_____

_____

_____

After you have finished, discuss your answers with another group. Which answers do your groups agree are the best? Which do your groups agree are the worst? Finally, perform a role play for the class. Choose one of the situations, and act it out. Would your attempt to start a conversation be successful? You decide.

Write about It

1. Tell a true or imaginary story about your experience with love at first sight.

2. Describe your ideal romantic partner.

3. Are you usually sensible or romantic?

People Say . . .

You can't judge a book by its cover. —Saying

You never get a second chance to make a first impression. —Saying

What do these sayings mean?

Do you know of similar sayings?

Vocabulary Review

1. Ann is short, but she wears high-heeled shoes to give people the

   _____ that she is taller.

2. My aunt has a dog and a cat who are very _____ . They never fight.

3. The teacher thought that the students wanted more homework. However, when

   he _____ them, he learned that they actually wanted less.

4. Molly chose her college because her favorite movie star had studied there.

   Emma was more _____ . She chose a college that offered many

   majors and had good professors.

5. My friend said she learned all of her English from listening to the radio.

   I'm _____ about that. I think she must have had some English

   classes, too.

Stories about Love at First Sight

(Activity 1)

Usually, I go to my favorite coffee shop on Sunday morning, get a cup of coffee, sit at a table, and read the newspaper. One day, I followed my usual routine, but something very special happened. I met the perfect woman. The coffee shop was very crowded, and there was only one empty table. I sat down at it and started to drink my coffee and read my newspaper. Then I heard a voice ask, "Do you mind if I sit down?" I looked up and saw a woman with sparkling eyes and a beautiful smile. I was attracted by more than her eyes and her smile, though. I also noticed that she was holding a copy of Shakespeare's *Hamlet,* my favorite play. I could tell that we had a lot in common. I had never seen her before, but I had a feeling that she was the right woman for me. It really was love at first sight.

Every year, my sister has a birthday party at her house. I went to my sister's party again this year, but I had an unexpected surprise. I met Jerry. I noticed him as soon as I walked in the door. He was sitting on the sofa and talking to my sister. Jerry and my sister hadn't noticed me come in, and they kept talking. Jerry was so handsome that I couldn't stop looking at him. My heart started to beat faster, and my knees felt weak. I had no idea who Jerry was, but I hoped that he wasn't my sister's boyfriend—or anyone else's boyfriend. Finally, I walked over and said hello to my sister, who introduced me to Jerry. The three of us talked together for a few minutes, and I found out that Jerry worked at the same company as my sister. Jerry told me a little bit about his job and his hometown, but I couldn't really concentrate on what he was saying. Even though he was right in front of me, his voice sounded far away. I had never experienced anything like that before. I knew that I was falling in love at first sight.

Answer Box

Activity 2

Score key

7–11   You could fall in love at first sight anywhere. If you're attracted to someone, you aren't shy about letting the person know. You fall in and out of love very easily. In fact, you might need to be a little less spontaneous.

12–16   You've fallen in love at first sight, but you know that sometimes love at first sight can end in disappointment. You don't want to be disappointed again, but don't give up. The perfect love could be waiting for you.

17–21   When you see the perfect person, your heart tells you to speak, but you're too shy. Maybe you're afraid of taking a risk. Go ahead. Maybe that perfect person is hoping that you'll say the first word.

19

Group Tour or Independent Travel?

Starting Off

1. Do you like to travel?

2. What is your most memorable vacation?

3. Who do you enjoy traveling with?

4. Where did you go on your last vacation?

Vocabulary

transportation—(noun) a method of carrying passengers or goods from one place to another

Most big cities offer many kinds of public **transportation** for people to get around.

The car is one of the most convenient methods of **transportation.**

book—(verb) arrange—with a hotel, restaurant, theater, etc., to go there at a particular time in the future

They **booked** their hotel room in advance, so they didn't have to worry about the chance of there being no room available.

Churches recommend that you **book** a wedding date at least six months in advance.

lonely—(adjective) feeling sad because you are alone

The new high school student felt a little **lonely** until she met some new friends.

Some older people who live alone tend to feel a little **lonely.**

stranger—(noun) a person whom you do not know

The mother yelled at her son when she found out he talked to a total **stranger.**

Nobody recognized the **strangers** walking around the building, so a security guard asked these people who they were.

destination—(noun) the place that someone or something is going to

After making a stop in Chicago, the final **destination** of the plane was Los Angeles.

When planning a vacation, it is important to first have a **destination** in mind.

19

Reading

Package vacations or group tours are extremely popular among tourists. Some people feel that it is worthwhile to have their whole trip planned out for them. Everything from **transportation** to food to lodging is taken care of by the tour operator. It is sometimes a relief to know that after a long day of sightseeing, a tour bus is waiting to take everyone to a hotel that has been **booked** in advance. Not only can package tours be cheaper than planning a trip independently, but it's almost impossible to feel **lonely** when traveling with a group.

▶ ▶ ▶ ▶ ▶ ▶ ▶

For some people, the thought of traveling with a group of **strangers** is not a pleasant way to spend vacation time. Planning a trip independently allows the tourists to see and do exactly what they want. It is also possible to change a particular **destination** after the trip has begun. People who travel independently also have more chances for direct contact with local people. If you know where you want to go and what you want to see and if you enjoy the planning process, independent travel may be for you.

Comprehension Questions

1. On a group tour, what do tourists do at the end of the day?

2. Who does all the planning on a group tour?

3. Who does all the planning for independent travel?

4. Which type of traveler has a greater chance for direct contact with the local people? Why?

Discussion Activities

Activity 1

In a small group, discuss the advantages and disadvantages of group tours and of independent travel. Write your answers in the chart that follows.

Advantages of Group Tours	Disadvantages of Group Tours

Advantages of Independent Travel	Disadvantages of Independent Travel

Charlie and Rosa want to take a vacation. They are thinking of going to Europe for a few weeks for the upcoming summer. They cannot decide if they should go on a group tour or plan their trip themselves and go independently. The class will form two groups and debate. Group A will try to convince Charlie and Rosa to go on a group tour. Group B will try to convince them that going independently is the best way. Make sure everyone has a chance to participate in the discussion.

Conversation Tip

When you want to give someone more information, you can use these expressions:

In other words, . . .

What I'm trying to say is . . .

A: Traveling with a group seems really stressful.

B: Don't you want to travel with other people?

A: The people don't bother me. It's the schedule. **In other words,** I feel more relaxed when I can decide my schedule by myself.

Language Learning Tip

When you see a word and you don't know how to say it, you can use this expression:

How do you say _____ ?

A: This tour looks interesting. **How do you say** the name of this city?

B: Oh, it's pronounced "Kuala Lumpur." It's in Malaysia.

Try to use these tips in your discussion.

Wrap Up

Which group was more convincing?

What were the strengths and weaknesses of each group's presentation?

What types of people do you think would choose a group tour?

What types of people do you think would choose to travel independently?

Activity 2

Work with a partner. You and your partner are travel agents. Plan trips for the following people. Decide if they should go on a group tour or travel independently. Figure out where they should go. Plan how much time they should spend on their vacation. Discuss the trip with your partner before writing down your ideas.

1. Dan and Bob have just graduated from college.

    Independent or group trip? _____

    Where? _____

    How long? _____

    Special considerations: _____

2. An elderly couple wants to celebrate their 50th wedding anniversary.

    Independent or group trip? _____

    Where? _____

    How long? _____

    Special considerations: _____

3. Mark and Sarah Smith want to take a vacation with their three young children.

    Independent or group trip? _____

    Where? _____

    How long? _____

    Special considerations: _____

4. Aressa is a 30-year-old lawyer who is exhausted.

    Independent or group trip? _____

    Where? _____

    How long? _____

    Special considerations: _____

5. Julie and Mike are getting married, and they want to plan a honeymoon.

Independent or group trip? _____

Where? _____

How long? _____

Special considerations: _____

You have been all over the world and have visited every continent. Now you want to take a more adventurous and unusual trip. Where will you go? Look at the following destinations. With a partner, decide if it would be better to go independently or with a group. Give one advantage and disadvantage for each method of travel.

1. The top of Mt. Everest

Independent: ____   Group: ____

Advantage: _____   Advantage: _____

Disadvantage: _____   Disadvantage: _____

2. The Amazon rain forest in Brazil

Independent: ____   Group: ____

Advantage: _____   Advantage: _____

Disadvantage: _____   Disadvantage: _____

3. Antarctica

Independent: ____   Group: ____

Advantage: _____   Advantage: _____

Disadvantage: _____   Disadvantage: _____

4. Sailing around the Greek islands

Independent: ____   Group: ____

Advantage: _____   Advantage: _____

Disadvantage: _____   Disadvantage: _____

5. Safari in Kenya

Independent: ____   Group: ____

Advantage: _____   Advantage: _____

Disadvantage: _____   Disadvantage: _____

6. _____ (Your turn. Write a destination)

Independent: ____   Group: ____

Advantage: _____   Advantage: _____

Disadvantage: _____   Disadvantage: _____

Write about It

1. If you could go anywhere in the world, where would you go? Why?

2. Which do you generally prefer, a group tour or an independent trip?

3. Describe your perfect vacation.

People Say . . .

The heaviest baggage for a traveler is an empty purse. —Saying

It's a nice place to visit, but I wouldn't want to live there. —Anonymous

What do these sayings mean?

Do you know of similar sayings?

Vocabulary Review

1. At a young age, children are taught that talking to _____ is dangerous.

2. The tourist _____ all of his hotel reservations before he went on vacation.

3. The high school students rely on bus _____ to get to and from school each day.

4. The train conductor announced that the final _____ would be Washington, D.C.

5. If you ever feel _____ , you can always call a friend.

20

Newspaper or TV News?

Starting Off

1. How do you get most of your news?

2. How has the way people get news changed in recent years?

3. How often do you read a newspaper?

4. How often do you read or watch news in English?

Vocabulary

enable—(verb) allow, make something possible

Olga's English ability **enabled** her to travel in the United States more easily.

Money **enables** you to buy many things, but it can't buy happiness.

update—(noun) new information

I want to give you an **update** on our meeting. It will be at nine o'clock instead of ten o'clock.

I never get **updates** from that department. I have no idea what they're doing these days.

still—(adjective) not moving

Danielle is so **still.** I think she's sleeping.

My son will never sit **still** during dinner. He's always trying to leave the table.

cover—(verb) report on, have information about

The first chapter of the book **covers** early American history.

I used to be a reporter. I **covered** town politics for a small newspaper.

perspective—(noun) point of view, opinion

Will and Paula always see things from different **perspectives.** They can never agree.

Mariko has lived in the United States for a long time, so she understands the American **perspective** on most issues.

Reading

These days, when news happens, people all over the world can learn about it almost immediately. Years ago, that wasn't possible, but television has changed everything. Modern technology **enables** us to sit at home and watch news taking place thousands of miles away instead of just reading about it. One of the biggest changes in TV news was the introduction of CNN, Cable News Network. CNN was founded by Ted Turner in 1980 and is based in Atlanta, Georgia, in the United States. CNN broadcasts news from around the world 24 hours a day, so viewers can get **updates** on a story at any time.

▷ ▷ ▷ ▷ ▷ ▷ ▷ ▷

Despite the popularity of TV, newspapers are still a very important source of news. In fact, *USA Today,* the largest American newspaper, sells more than two million copies a day. With a newspaper, you can only read about a story after it has taken place, and you can only see **still** photographs. However, newspapers usually **cover** stories in much more detail than TV news does. In a newspaper, there may be several articles on the same piece of news, and these articles are often written from different **perspectives.** This gives the reader a good understanding of the important issues in the story. Because a newspaper is printed, it is also possible to go back and check any parts of the story that you didn't understand. This is not an option with TV news.

Comprehension Questions

1. How has television changed the way that people get their news? Give two answers.

2. What is the difference between CNN and most other TV stations?

3. What are two disadvantages of newspapers?

4. What are two advantages of newspapers?

Discussion Activities

Activity 1

In a small group, discuss the advantages and disadvantages of newspapers and of TV news. Write your ideas in the chart that follows.

Advantages of Newspapers	Disadvantages of Newspapers

Advantages of TV News	Disadvantages of TV News

A UFO landed in Washington, D.C., last night and is parked in front of the White House. The aliens in it have said that they will not leave until the president personally delivers to them 10,000 cans of green beans. (They like green beans for some reason.) Lucy can get news about the story from either the newspaper or the TV. The class will form two groups and debate. Group A will try to convince Lucy to read the newspaper for her information on the story. Group B will try to convince her to watch the news on TV. During this discussion, make sure that everyone has a chance to speak.

Conversation Tip

When you want to disagree and add your own opinion, you can use these expressions:

I see what you mean, but . . .

That's a good point, but . . .

A: The six o'clock news is great because I can watch it while I'm eating dinner.

B: **That's a good point, but** some people are never home at that time.

Language Learning Tip

If you don't understand what people say because they speak too quickly, you can use this expression:

A: According to the newspaper, crime has decreased this year.

B: **Would you mind saying that again more slowly?**

A: I said that crime has decreased, according to the newspaper.

Try to use these tips in your discussion.

Wrap Up

1. Which group was more convincing?

2. What were the strengths and weaknesses of each group's presentation?

Activity 2

Many TV news stories are reported with a news anchor (who sits at a desk in the TV studio), a field reporter (who reports from the scene of the news), and a witness (who saw the news event take place and is being interviewed by the reporter). In a group of three, discuss a news event that you would like to report on. You may choose an important event in the world or one that is happening at your school.

You can even make up a story. Write down a script for your news report. Try to give each member of your group about the same number of lines. Finally, perform your report for a group of classmates, or videotape your report and show the class your video.

Activity 3

Many newspapers try to attract readers by using exciting photos on the front page. Some photographers will do almost anything to get such a photo. However, there are "invasion of privacy" laws in the United States to protect people from being bothered. For example, a photographer can take a movie star's picture when the star is appearing at the Academy Awards show. However, the photographer cannot walk into the star's house without his or her permission and take his or her picture. That would be an invasion of the star's privacy. These two situations are easy to understand, but there are some that are not as clear. In a small group, discuss the three situations that follow. Explain why you think they are or are not invasions of privacy. Talk about your answers with the class. Then look at the answers at the end of this chapter.

Situation 1
A well-known football player wanted to ask his girlfriend to marry him. He took her to the park where they first met and waited until he didn't see anyone else around. Then he gave her a diamond ring and proposed to her. She accepted but asked him not to tell anyone about their engagement because she was a very private person. He agreed to keep it a secret. While this was happening, a photographer was hiding behind a tree. He took their picture and sold it to a newspaper.

Situation 2
Same as situation 1, but the couple was in the man's apartment, standing near a window. The photographer was on the sidewalk, saw them through the window, and took a picture.

Situation 3
Same as situation 2, but the photographer couldn't see much from the sidewalk, so she used a camera with a high-powered telephoto lens.

Write about It

1. Describe a recent news story and tell why you think it was important.

2. What is the difference between news coverage in the United States and the coverage in other countries?

3. How could news coverage be improved?

People Say . . .

No news is good news. —Saying

Good news travels fast. —Saying

What do these sayings mean?

Do you know of similar sayings?

Vocabulary Review

1. Sophie is French, and Ed is American. They are both reporters, but they often write from different _____ .

2. I never use a video camera when I'm on vacation. I prefer to take _____ photographs.

3. Some people like video because it _____ you to see movement.

4. I just got an _____ on Angela's new baby. He's healthy and can leave the hospital tomorrow.

5. American newspapers don't _____ news in my country very much. Fortunately, I can get that news from the Internet.

Answer Box

Activity 3

Invasion of Privacy

According to U.S. law, situation 1 is not an invasion of privacy, because the park is a public place. It is true that the photographer hid behind a tree, but anyone walking by could have seen the couple.

Situation 2 is not an invasion of privacy. It is similar to situation 1. The man's apartment is a private place, but anyone walking by could have seen the couple through the window.

Situation 3 is an invasion of privacy. No one walking by could have seen the couple. The photographer could see them only because she was using a high-powered telephoto lens. The couple had no reason to believe that other people could see them.

21

Cats or Dogs?

Starting Off

1. Do you have a pet? If so, what kind?

2. What are the most popular kinds of pets people have in your country?

3. Do you think it is better to buy a pet or to adopt a pet from a shelter?

4. What are some unusual pets people keep?

Vocabulary

conduct—(verb) do something to get information or to prove a fact

The school system **conducted** a survey to see how many different languages students spoke at home.

The scientists spent years **conducting** tests to make sure the new medication was safe.

morale—(noun) level of confidence and positive feelings, usually among a group

After the football team won the championship, the **morale** of the team went up.

Successful companies usually have high **morale.**

tolerate—(verb) be able to accept something unpleasant or difficult

The school does not **tolerate** any violence among its students.

His allergies were so severe that he could not **tolerate** being outside.

fond—(adjective) liking someone or something very much

He is **fond** of chocolate.

Growing up, she was never very **fond** of sports, but now she participates on two teams a year.

groom —(verb) take care of one's appearance

Some animals spend a lot of time **grooming** themselves.

Before going out on a big date, Matt will **groom** himself in front of the mirror.

Reading

Many people think that a dog is man's best friend. Dogs are loyal and generally become important members of the family. According to the Food Marketing Institute, there are 61 million dogs in the United States. The American Pet Association **conducted** a survey that found that four million dog owners are as attached to their dogs as they are to their spouses. Did you know that some dog owners occasionally take their dogs to work? One company owner found that once he allowed employees to take their dogs to work, **morale** and attendance improved. Maybe a dog *is* "man's best friend"!

▷ ▷ ▷ ▷ ▷ ▷ ▷

Other people cannot **tolerate** dogs. Some of these people are very **fond** of cats. It is estimated that there are 500 million domestic cats in the world. In America alone, there are 74 million cats. Cats are known to "read" your moods, so if you are feeling sad or depressed, your cat's behavior may change. If you look into the eyes of a cat, its pupils will change according to its mood. Cats also have an amazing hearing ability and can recognize their owner's footsteps hundreds of feet away. Cleanliness is very important to cats, so they spend 30 percent of their time **grooming** themselves. They may not be "man's best friend," but they certainly are clean!*

Comprehension Questions

1. How many dogs are there in the United States?

2. What are the benefits when employees take their dogs to work?

3. How many cats are there in the United States?

4. What percentage of their time do cats spend grooming themslves?

---

*Information from American Pet Association, http://www.apapets.com/petstats2.htm, accessed August 20, 2003; from http://www.flippyscatpage.com, accessed February 20, 2003; and from http://www.geocities.com/Heartland/2321/trivia.htm, accessed August 20, 2003.

Discussion Activities

Activity 1

In a small group, discuss the advantages and disadvantages of having cats and dogs as pets. Write your answers in the chart that follows.

Advantages of Cats as Pets	Disadvantages of Cats as Pets

Advantages of Dogs as Pets	Disadvantages of Dogs as Pets

Michael has just moved to New York City. After living in an apartment where pets were not allowed, he is finally allowed to have one. Growing up, he had both cats and dogs, and he likes both animals. He can't decide if he should get a cat or a dog. The class will form two groups and debate. Group A will try to convince Michael that he should get a cat. Group B will try to convince him that getting a dog is the best idea. Make sure everyone has a chance to participate in the discussion.

Conversation Tip

When you want to show that you agree with someone, you can use these expressions:

I agree.

That's right.

A: Cats are so much easier to care for than dogs.

B: **That's right.** That's why I got a cat instead of a dog.

Language Learning Tip

When you aren't sure how to spell a word, you can use this expression:

How do you spell that?

A: Sandra just got a new cat. I think it's a Siamese.

B: Siamese? **How do you spell that?**

A: S-I-A-M-E-S-E.

Try to use these tips in your discussion.

Wrap Up

Which group was more convincing?

What were the strengths and weakness of each group's presentation?

Activity 2

Working in small groups, you have to figure out which pet would be better for the people in each scenario. Give a few reasons why you chose the animal you did for each situation. Be ready to discuss your answers with the rest of the class when you have finished.

Situation 1

Sara is a 34-year-old professional. She lives in the city and rarely goes away. She lives in an apartment on a busy street.

Animal _____ Why? _____

Situation 2

Bob and Stacy live in the suburbs. Stacy is a doctor, and Bob is a stay-at-home dad. They have three children, ages 5, 7, and 9. They usually go on weekend trips to the country. Bob's parents live down the street.

Animal _____ Why? _____

Situation 3

Joe lives in the city. He is a salesman and travels around the country a few weekends a month, selling computer products. There is a nice park in front of his apartment building.

Animal _____ Why? _____

Situation 4

Larry lives in a large apartment building. He is 78 years old and is in pretty good health. He goes away for one week every summer.

Animal _____ Why? _____

Activity 3

Following the models in activity 2, write your own scenario to share with your classmates. Work in a small group. Include the name and age of each person in your scenario. Also mention the living situation of the person or persons.

Your Situation

Name(s) of person(s): _____

Age(s) of person(s): _____

Living situation: _____

Write about It

1. In elementary schools in the United States, it is common for classrooms to have a pet. It may be a hamster, fish, or bird. Were there pets in your elementary school? If not, can you explain why?

2. In the United States, there are many shelters for homeless animals. People can adopt a cat or dog from one of these places. Do you know of a similar system that exists elsewhere? Explain how you would acquire a pet.

3. Some pet lovers bury their pets in pet cemeteries when they die. Do you know of such customs?

People Say . . .

A dog is man's best friend. —Saying

When I play with my cat, who knows if I am not a pastime to her more than she is to me. —Montaigne, French philosopher and essayist

What do these sayings mean?

Do you know of similar sayings?

Vocabulary Review

1. Thomas is a very light sleeper, so he cannot _____ all the noise his neighbors make.

2. Gorillas spend much of the day _____ each other.

3. When the employees heard that the company might close, the _____ went down.

4. Most children are very _____ of sweets.

5. The mayor of the city _____ a survey to see how popular she was with the local people.

Some English or All English?

Starting Off

1. What has most helped you improve your English?

2. What has prevented you from improving your English more?

3. How often do you speak English outside of class?

4. What is the longest time you have spoken only English?

Vocabulary

devote—(verb) use for a special purpose, give one's time and energy

> To become an Olympic athlete, you must **devote** every day to training for your sport.

> Dr. Conners **devoted** his life to teaching. He was the best professor I ever had.

dilemma—(noun) problem, difficult situation

> Laura has a **dilemma.** She wants to lose weight, but she loves sweets.

> Ted likes the beach, but his wife likes the mountains. For them, planning a vacation is a real **dilemma.**

institute—(verb) start, begin to use

> I wasn't required to take that exam in order to graduate high school. The exam was **instituted** the year after I graduated.

> No smoking is allowed in the restaurant. This rule was **instituted** five years ago.

policy—(noun) rule, idea about a certain issue

> Ten years ago, you could smoke in that restaurant. Now it has a no-smoking **policy.**

> The president's **policies** were popular. Most people agreed with them.

universally—(adverb) completely, widely

> The movie was **universally** popular. Everybody loved it.

> My mother's tomato soup is **universally** hated in my family. It's awful.

Reading

Every year, thousands of students from all over the world go abroad to study English. They may spend 25 hours a week in class and **devote** time each day to homework. When they go outside, they are surrounded by native English speakers. Yet one of the most common complaints of these students is, "I don't have enough opportunity to speak English." Although these students are living in an English-speaking country, they often become friends with classmates who share their native language. This creates a **dilemma,** because these students may spend the majority of their out-of-class time conversing in their first language. As a result, they miss valuable opportunities to practice what they've studied in class, and their English doesn't improve as quickly as they would like it to.

▸ ▸ ▸ ▸ ▸ ▸ ▸

Some language programs have **instituted** rules to increase the amount of English spoken by students. The schools require their students to speak only English in some or all of the school buildings. According to some **policies,** students must speak English, even in the dormitories. These policies may force students to speak more English. However, they are not **universally** popular with students. Some students complain that they need at least some time to speak their own language, instead of struggling with English all day and night. English-only rules may solve the problem of lack of English practice. Unfortunately, the rules may lead to another problem—too much English.

Comprehension Questions

1. Why do students studying English abroad spend so much time speaking their native language?

2. What is the disadvantage of speaking one's native language outside of class?

3. How do some schools try to make their students speak more English outside of class?

4. Why do some students complain about having to speak only English?

Discussion Activities

Activity 1

In a small group, talk about the advantages and disadvantages of language policies. Write your answers in the chart that follows.

Advantages of English-Only Policies	Disadvantages of English-Only Policies
Advantages of Having No Language Policy	**Disadvantages of Having No Language Policy**

The teachers at the English Institute want their students to speak more English. Therefore, the teachers are thinking about instituting an English-only policy. The class will form two groups and debate. Group A will try to convince the teachers that such a policy would be a good idea. Group B will try to convince the teachers that the English-only policy would be a mistake. During this discussion, make sure that everyone has a chance to speak.

Conversation Tip

When you want to show that you disagree with someone, you can use these expressions:

I disagree.

I don't think so.

A: I think students should be required to speak English in the cafeteria.

B: **I don't think so.** I think we should be able to relax and speak our own language during lunch.

Language Learning Tip

When you don't understand what someone said, you can use this expression:

Could you say that again?

A: At my old language school, they instituted an English-only policy.

B: **Could you say that again?**

A: At my old language school, we had to speak English all the time.

Try to use these tips in your discussion.

Wrap Up

Which group was more convincing?

What were the strengths and weaknesses of each group's presentation?

Activity 2

In a small group, talk about other policies that an English language program might institute to help its students improve their English. List three of your ideas here, along with the advantages and disadvantages of each policy?

Policy 1: _____

Advantages	Disadvantages

Policy 2: _____

Advantages	Disadvantages

Policy 3: _____

Advantages	Disadvantages

Activity 3

Pedro and Luis are studying English abroad and are roommates. They are both native Spanish speakers, but Pedro wants to speak English all the time, even in their room. Luis doesn't want to speak English with native Spanish speakers. What kind of agreement do you think they can reach? Discuss this question with a partner.

After you have decided what Pedro and Luis will do, perform a role play in which you and your partner play the roles of the roommates. In the role play, the two of you should discuss the dilemma and your solution to it.

Write about It

1. Imagine that a native English speaker is going to study abroad. What advice would you give that person to help him or her learn the host country's language?

2. Has learning English changed the way you think about another language? How?

3. Imagine that you are an English teacher. Describe your special teaching method.

People Say . . .

When in Rome, do as the Romans do. —Saying

What we learn to do, we learn by doing. —Aristotle, Greek philosopher

What do these sayings mean?

Do you know of similar sayings?

Vocabulary Review

1. People can buy that medicine anywhere in the world. It's _____ available.

2. You can't bring your dog into this store. That's our _____ .

3. I want to invite two friends to the game, but I only have one extra ticket. It's a big _____ .

4. My company _____ a new rule. Now no one can wear jeans to work.

5. Ralph works in a bookstore during the day, but he _____ his nights to music. He plays with his band several nights a week.

23

Cash or Credit?

Starting Off

1. How many credit cards do you have?

2. How often do you charge items?

3. What is the cheapest item you have ever charged?

4. Do you prefer to carry cash or credit cards with you?

Vocabulary

purchase—(verb) buy

He decided to **purchase** a new car next month.

The woman asked me where I **purchased** my handbag.

bankruptcy—(noun) the state of not being able to pay your debts

After three years of losing money, the company filed for **bankruptcy.**

When the economy goes down, **bankruptcy** cases increase.

perk—(noun) something you get (usually from a job) in addition to what is expected

She took the job because of all the **perks** she was offered.

It is uncommon to receive **perks** if you aren't working full-time.

debt—(noun) an amount of money you owe

Because he used his charge card too often, he had a lot of **debt.**

If you stay on a budget, it is easy to avoid getting into **debt.**

cancel—(verb) end an agreement that exists

She wants to **cancel** her magazine subscription, because it's getting too expensive.

Because of an illness in the family, they had to **cancel** their vacation.

Reading

Some people believe that if you can't pay cash for something, you should wait to buy it when you can. These people choose to **purchase** most or all of their things using cash. According to David and Tom Gardner, 1.3 million credit card holders in the United States are declaring **bankruptcy.*** Using cash usually forces a person to follow a budget so that all expenses can be covered from month to month. All of the money that would go to pay for interest on a credit card balance can be invested instead.

---

*Information from The Motley Fool, http://www.fool.com, accessed January 15, 2003.

▷▷▷▷▷▷▷

Carrying a credit card can make life very convenient. Using a credit card allows the user to develop a good credit history. In addition, many credit card companies offer **perks**—such as airline miles or cash back—if you use their cards. The average American household has about $8,500 in credit card **debt,**[*] so credit cards are being used all of the time. If you lose your credit card, it is very easy to **cancel** it. If you lose your cash, you may as well kiss it good-bye!

Comprehension Questions

1. How many credit card holders in the United States are declaring bankruptcy?

2. Why do people choose to use cash when purchasing items?

3. What are two perks that credit card companies offer to people who charge items?

4. How much credit card debt does the average American household carry?

Discussion Activities

Activity 1

Discuss the advantages and disadvantages of using cash and of using credit cards. Write your answers in the chart that follows.

---

[*]Information from The Motley Fool, http://www.fool.com, accessed January 15, 2003.

Advantages of Using Cash	Disadvantages of Using Cash
Advantages of Using Credit Cards	**Disadvantages of Using Credit Cards**

Tamara is going off to college in a few months. Her father thinks she should have a credit card for emergency use. Her mother thinks that having a credit card will mean big trouble for Tamara. The class will form two groups and debate. Group A will try to convince the family that Tamara should only have cash when she's away at college. Group B will try to convince the family that having a credit card is a good idea. During this discussion, make sure that everyone has a chance to speak.

Conversation Tip

When you want to ask for more information, you can use these expressions:

Can you explain that?

What do you mean exactly?

A: Sometimes credit cards can be dangerous.

B: **What do you mean exactly?**

A: Well, if you charge more than you can afford, you'll end up paying a lot of interest.

Language Learning Tip

When you don't understand a word, you can use this expression:

What does _____ mean?

A: My roommate got into a lot of debt with her credit card.

B: Debt? **What does that mean?**

A: It means "the amount of money you owe."

Try to use these tips in your discussion.

Wrap Up

Which group was more convincing?

What were the strengths and weaknesses of each group's presentation?

Activity 2

Look at the following list. Is it better to use cash to purchase the items? Or is it better to charge the items? Please explain how you came up with your answers. First, work alone. Then, discuss your answers with a partner.

Item	Cash	Charge	Why?
Airline ticket	___	___	_____
Groceries	___	___	_____
Shoes	___	___	_____
Textbooks	___	___	_____
Medical bill	___	___	_____
Fast-food meal	___	___	_____
Meal at a fancy restaurant	___	___	_____
Monthly car payment	___	___	_____
Rent	___	___	_____
School tuition	___	___	_____
Movie ticket	___	___	_____

Activity 3

The ways we use money to buy things are changing all the time. Some people use cash, and others choose to use credit cards. Work in pairs or small groups and discuss how money was used in the past, how it is used now, and how you think it will be used in the future.

Methods of using money 100 years ago

_____

_____

_____

Methods of using money now

_____

_____

_____

Methods of using money in 100 years

_____

_____

_____

How have the methods of using money changed over the years?

What is your favorite method of using money? Why?

How do you think we will be using money in the future? Do you think cash will still exist?

Write about It

1. Describe a time you decided to save your money to buy something. How long did it take you to save up the money? How old were you? What did you buy?

2. What are some items that you would never charge? What are your reasons for not charging them?

3. In the United States, it is very easy to get a credit card. What do you think it is like to get a credit card in other countries?

People Say . . .

Never spend money before you have it.
—Thomas Jefferson, American President

Beware of too great a bargain. —Saying

What do these sayings mean?

Do you know of similar sayings?

Vocabulary Review

1. Barbara decided to _____ her credit cards because she was using them more than she wanted.

2. The company filed for _____ because it lost too much money.

3. Before you _____ a new computer, you should research all the different models.

4. John doesn't make much money, but his employer gives him great _____ , including free meals and a cell phone with unlimited minutes.

5. Because of her school loans, she had a lot of _____ by the time she graduated.

Living in Luxury or Roughing It?

Starting Off

1. What do you do during your vacations?

2. Tell your classmates about a time you went camping or hiking.

3. Tell your classmates about a time you stayed in a hotel.

4. Do you prefer indoor activities or outdoor activities?

Vocabulary

luxury—(noun) comfort, especially because of having expensive things

> The king's family lives in **luxury.** They can buy anything they want.

> When my grandparents first came to the United States, they thought it was a land of **luxury,** because everyone seemed so rich.

folks—(noun) people, parents

> The **folks** at my company are very friendly. I like working with them.

> I lived with my **folks** until I was 21. Then I got my own apartment.

rough it—(phrasal verb) live without comforts

> My brother likes to **rough it** when he goes on vacation. He'd rather sleep on the ground than in a bed.

> After **roughing it** for a week, I wanted to go home, take a shower, and do my laundry.

pamper—(verb) give someone a lot of attention or things, often too much or too many

> The Smiths **pamper** their daughter. If she asks for something, they give it to her.

> When I want to **pamper** myself, I spend the day shopping and get a massage.

self-sufficient—(adjective) independent, able to do things by oneself

> Ian is very **self-sufficient.** He doesn't need help from anyone.

> We grow our own food and produce our own electricity. We are very **self-sufficient.**

Reading

There are all kinds of vacations. Some people like to spend their time off in **luxury** and might stay at a fancy hotel. Other **folks** enjoy **roughing it** and might prefer to go camping. People who like luxury might say that they work hard all year and want to **pamper** themselves when they are on vacation. At a nice hotel, they don't need to worry about cooking or cleaning up after themselves like they do at home. A hotel might even have special facilities like a swimming pool or hair salon. Of course, all this luxury comes at a price. The most stressful part of the vacation might be when it's time to pay the bill.

▷ ▷ ▷ ▷ ▷ ▷ ▷

A week of roughing it, by comparison, is very cheap. If you spend your days hiking and your nights sleeping in a tent, you just need some basic equipment and some food. Once you have used the equipment, you can continue to use it for many years. Roughing it also gives you a chance to challenge yourself by seeing how **self-sufficient** you can be. When you have to cook your own food, find your own water, and carry your own backpack, you may develop a new feeling of power. Or you may develop a dislike of roughing it and start thinking about a hot shower and a warm bed.

Comprehension Questions

1. Why do some people think they should pamper themselves on vacation?

2. Why might staying at a hotel be less stressful than staying home?

3. What are two reasons that roughing it might be better than spending a vacation in luxury?

4. What might happen if you don't enjoy roughing it?

Discussion Activities

Activity 1

In two groups, discuss the advantages and disadvantages of living in luxury and of roughing it. Write your answers in the chart that follows.

Advantages of Luxury	Disadvantages of Luxury

Advantages of Roughing It	Disadvantages of Roughing It

Imagine that your class is going to take a vacation. There are two options, living in luxury and roughing it. The class will form two groups and debate. Group A will try to convince the class that a vacation of luxury would be better. Group B will try to convince the class that a vacation of roughing it would be better. During the discussion, make sure that everyone has a chance to speak.

Conversation Tip

When you want to give someone more information, you can use these expressions:

What I mean is . . .

For example, . . .

A: I like camping more than anything else.

B: More than your mother?

A: No, seriously. **What I mean is** that I think camping is the best way to spend a vacation.

Language Learning Tip

When you see a word and you don't know how to say it, you can use this expression:

How do you pronounce _____ ?

A: Look at the name of this hotel. How do you pronounce it?

B: "S-T period" is pronounced "Saint," so it's "Saint Moritz."

Try to use these tips in your discussion.

Wrap Up

Which group was more convincing?

What were the strengths and weaknesses of each group's presentation?

It is summertime, and you are planning to spend the weekend hiking and camping in the mountains. What 20 items will you bring? Talk to a partner and write your answers below. Then check the list at the end of the chapter. Finally, discuss your answers with the class. What is on the list that you didn't plan to bring? What did you plan to bring that isn't on the list?

Camping Gear

1.
2.
3.
4.
5.
6.
7.
8.
9.
10.
11.
12.
13.
14.
15.
16.
17.
18.
19.
20.

Activity 3

Work with a partner. Imagine that you both work for a travel agency. Discuss what kind of package tour you would offer your customers. Provide for either a week of living in luxury or a week of roughing it. Write down the details of your tour and present your idea to the class.

Write about It

1. Do you know anyone who lives in luxury? Describe a day in his or her life.

2. What is one type of roughing it that you would never do? Why not?

3. What do you do when you want to pamper yourself?

People Say . . .

A field that has rested gives a bountiful crop. —Ovid, Roman poet

Simplicity is the peak of civilization. —Jessie Sampter, American author

What do these sayings mean?

Do you know of similar sayings?

Vocabulary Review

1. When I was growing up, I had to work for everything. My parents never _____ me.

2. Ben was a famous movie star, and his life was filled with _____ . He had expensive cars, several vacation homes, and his own plane.

3. A _____ country can produce everything it needs.

4. I'm not interested in hiking up a mountain or sleeping outside. I don't want to

_____ .

5. My friends' parents bought them cars, but my _____ bought me

a bicycle.

Answer Box

Activity 2

Camping Gear

1. camp stove
2. cookware/pots, pans, and utensils
3. day pack/backpack
4. extra clothes
5. first-aid kit
6. flashlight/headlamp
7. food
8. fuel for camp stove
9. garbage bags (for trash and for lining your day pack in case of rain)
10. hiking boots
11. insect repellent
12. pocket knife
13. rain gear/raincoat and rain pants
14. sleeping bag
15. sunscreen
16. tent
17. toilet paper
18. water
19. water-purification tablets
20. waterproof matches

Renting an Apartment or Buying a Condominium?

Starting Off

1. Would you prefer to live in an apartment or a condominium?

2. What do you think is a reasonable amount to pay for apartment rent?

3. What are the responsibilities of a landlord?

4. Have you ever had a really good or really bad landlord? Explain.

Vocabulary

mobility—(noun) the ability to move easily from one place to another

Young people have much more **mobility** than older people.

Some jobs require people to have a lot of **mobility.**

mortgage—(noun) a legal arrangement with a bank, in which a person borrows money (usually for a house) and pays it back over a number of years

The young couple decided they could afford a monthly **mortgage,** so they bought a house.

Some people work two jobs to pay the monthly **mortgage.**

landlord—(noun) a person who rents a room, apartment, or building to someone else

The **landlord** wanted the tenants to pay their rent on the first day of every month.

If there are problems with the heat in your apartment, you should call the **landlord.**

condominium—(noun) a building that consists of separate units, each of which is owned by the people living in it

The couple couldn't afford a house, so they decided to buy a **condominium.**

In addition to a mortgage, people living in a **condominium** have to pay a monthly condominium fee.

investment—(noun) the money people put into a company, business, or bank to make a profit

She made a bad **investment** by putting all of her money into the stock market.

Some people pay for financial advice to learn how to make a good **investment.**

25

Reading

For those who need a lot of convenience and **mobility,** renting an apartment is an attractive option to buying a **condominium.** People who live in an apartment avoid the monthly condominium fee. When a person considers the monthly **mortgage,** maintenance costs, and yearly taxes involved in buying a condominium, it is possible that renting may end up costing less from month to month. People who rent have little or no responsibilities when it comes to maintenance. If a pipe bursts, instead of having to worry about it, a renter just has to call the **landlord.**

▷▷▷▷▷▷▷

For others, buying a condominium or house and staying in one place is very important. Even though a condominium may look like an apartment, the condominium owner is building equity each month. If need be, the condominium owner can sell the property and make some money. In addition, the condominium owner is not dependent on a landlord for maintenance issues. The owner doesn't have to get permission to change the interior. For someone who wants to make an **investment** and finds owning a big house too overwhelming, buying a condominium may be the perfect solution.

Comprehension Questions

1. What are three things that a condominium owner has to worry about?

2. What does a renter do if a pipe bursts?

3. What are the advantages of owning a condominium over renting an apartment?

4. Why is buying a condominium considered an investment?

Discussion Activities

Activity 1

In a small group, discuss the advantages and disadvantages of renting an apartment and of buying a condominium. Write your answers in the chart that follows.

Advantages of Renting an Apartment	Disadvantages of Renting an Apartment
Advantages of Buying a Condominium	Disadvantages of Buying a Condominium

Yumiko is from Japan and wants to study in the United States for four years. After her studies, she may return to her country, or she may stay in the United States to work. She can't decide if she should rent an apartment or buy a condominium. The class will form two groups and debate. Group A will try to convince Yumiko to rent an apartment. Group B will try to convince Yumiko to buy a condominium. Make sure everyone has a chance to participate in the debate.

Conversation Tip

When you want to disagree and add your own opinion, you can use these expressions:

I know what you're saying, but . . .

That may be true, but . . .

A: Buying a condominium makes much more sense than paying rent every month.

B: **That may be true, but** you can't buy one without a down payment.

Language Learning Tip

If you don't understand what someone has said because he or she spoke too quickly, you can use this expression:

Could you speak more slowly?

Try to use these tips in your discussion.

Wrap Up

Which group was more convincing?

What were the strengths and weaknesses of each group's presentation?

Activity 2

Look at the following list of problems that can happen in an apartment. Who is responsible for taking care of these problems? First, answer by yourself. Then, work with a partner or in a small group and compare your answers. When you are finished, add a few additional apartment problems to the list.

Problem	Renter	Landlord
Broken pipe	___	___
Ripped window shade	___	___

Problem	Renter	Landlord
Mice in the apartment	——	——
Hot water is cold	——	——
Snow needs to be shoveled	——	——
Garbage needs to be removed	——	——
Bedroom needs to be painted	——	——
Ripped shower curtain	——	——
Locks need to be changed	——	——
Broken window	——	——
_____	——	——
_____	——	——

Activity 3

With a partner, discuss experiences you or someone you know has had with renting an apartment. These may be good experiences, or they may be bad experiences. In the space provided, write down a few of these stories. When you are finished, share one of your partner's stories with the class.

My Renting Stories   **My Partner's Renting Stories**

_____   _____

_____   _____

_____   _____

_____   _____

_____   _____

_____   _____

_____   _____

_____   _____

Write about It

1. Describe your "dream home."

2. Discuss at least three important things someone needs before he or she purchases a home.

3. In your opinion, is it better to rent or to own? Why?

People Say . . .

Every bird loves its own nest. —Saying

The borrower is the slave of the lender. —Saying

What do these sayings mean?

Do you know of similar sayings?

Vocabulary Review

1. The _____ knew that the couple didn't have a lot of money, so he took $50 off the rent.

2. Sara thought putting money in a new company was a risky _____ , so she opened a savings account instead.

3. If you are late paying your _____ , the bank will probably charge an additional fee.

4. He didn't want to live in a house by himself, so he bought a _____ .

5. Having a car gives us much more _____ for getting around.

Tipping **or** No Tipping?

Starting Off

1. When do people tip?

2. What do you think are the most confusing issues concerning tipping?

3. Do you think tipping affects the quality of service in a restaurant?

4. How was the service the last time you went to a restaurant?

Vocabulary

run into—(phrasal verb) meet or experience accidentally

I **ran into** an old friend of mine at the party. I was very surprised to see him there.

The weather doesn't look good. If you drive home now, you might **run into** a storm.

server—(noun) waiter or waitress, someone who serves food at a restaurant

The **server** made a mistake and brought me the wrong food.

If you don't understand the menu, ask the **server** to explain it to you.

party—(noun) group, especially in a restaurant

We had a **party** of eight, so we needed a big table.

That **party** arrived before us. After the server takes their order, she will take ours.

gratuity—(noun) tip, money (beyond a fee) that you give someone for a service

Everyone liked the restaurant's food, so they left a large **gratuity.**

The bill was $18.00. I only had $20, so I left a $2.00 **gratuity,** though I wanted to leave more.

wind up—(phrasal verb) finally do something, finally become

You need to sleep more, eat better food, and work less. If you don't, you'll **wind up** getting sick.

I couldn't understand the map you gave me. I drove around for an hour and **wound up** lost.

Reading

Most people don't realize how many confusing customs there are in other countries—until they travel abroad. Then, they **run into** situations that confuse even the natives. In the United States, one such custom is tipping. At certain times, customers are expected to tip, but the amount they tip is not set. At a restaurant, it is customary to tip the **server** 15–20 percent of the bill. People might choose to leave more or less, depending on the quality of the service.

▶ ▶ ▶ ▶ ▶ ▶ ▶

Some people tip roughly the same percentage every time they go out to eat. If people do that, you might think, restaurants should just include the tip as part of the bill. Sometimes restaurants do exactly that. Usually, this happens with large **parties,** for example, of eight or more people. If people go out to dinner in a large group, they might see "**Gratuity** 18%" or something similar written on their bill. If customers don't notice when a tip is included, they might **wind up** paying two gratuities. But they shouldn't feel bad. They'll make the server happy, and they won't be the first people confused by the American way of tipping.

Comprehension Questions

1. When do most people see that foreign countries have many customs that are difficult to understand?

2. How much do most Americans tip at a restaurant?

3. When might a restaurant include a tip on the bill?

4. Why might some people leave two tips?

Discussion Activities

Activity 1

Do you think people should tip at restaurants and other businesses, or do you think businesses should include tipping as part of the bill? In a small group, discuss the advantages and disadvantages of tipping. Write your answers in the chart that follows.

Advantages of Tipping	Disadvantages of Tipping

Imagine that you and your classmates are attending a meeting of the Restaurant Owners Association of America. The association is discussing whether to end the custom of tipping. The class will form two groups and debate. Group A will try to convince the association that it should keep the custom. Group B will try to convince the association to end tipping. Make sure that everyone has a chance to speak during the debate.

Conversation Tip

When you want to show that you agree with someone, you can use these expressions:

> **Exactly.**

> **That's for sure.**

A: Tipping in America is really confusing.

B: **That's for sure.** We never tip in my country.

Language Learning Tip

When you aren't sure how to spell a word, you can use this expression:

> **Could you spell that for me?**

A: What's that word we learned that means "tip"?

B: Oh, I think you mean "gratuity."

A: Yeah, that's it. **Could you spell that for me?**

B: No problem. You spell it G-R-A-T-U-I-T-Y.

Try to use these tips in your discussion.

Wrap Up

Which group was more convincing?

What were the strengths and weaknesses of each group's presentation?

Look at the situations below. Working with a partner, try to guess which situations require tipping in the United States and which do not. Either practice may apply in some situations.

1. You're sitting at a table. You order a drink from the server.

2. You're standing at a bar. You order a beer from the bartender.

3. A salesperson at a store helps you choose some clothes.

4. You get a haircut at a salon.

5. You pick up your clothes at the dry cleaner's.

6. You order a pizza, and someone delivers it to your house.

7. You take a taxi to the airport.

8. A porter takes your bag from the taxi into the airport.

9. An usher at the movies helps you find a seat.

10. A gas station attendant puts gas in your car.

Discuss your answers as a class, then look at the answers at the end of this chapter. With your partner, discuss the difference between tipping in the United States and tipping in another country with which you are familiar. Which system do you like better?

Restaurants want to know what their customers think about the food, the service, etc. If a restaurant knows, it can improve these things. In order to find out, many restaurants use "comment cards." These are cards that are put on the tables or given to the customers by their servers. The cards ask the customers various questions about the restaurant. These may be yes/no questions (*Was your server polite?*), information questions (*What did you like most about the food?*), or questions that are answered on a scale (*How would you rate the food? Circle one answer: 1   2   3   4   5*). In the last type of question, usually *1* means *terrible,* and *5* means *excellent.*

With a partner, make a list of questions for a comment card. Try to make at least 10 questions, and try to use all three of the question types listed. After you have finished, discuss your comment cards with the class. The class should vote on the best questions from each card and put these questions on the board. Using the questions on the board, the class should then discuss some local restaurants. How would your classmates rate these restaurants? How could the restaurants be improved?

Write about It

1. Imagine that you are opening a new business (restaurant, hotel, store, etc.). Describe what type of service you will give the customers. What will make your business better than other, similar businesses?

2. Describe a very good experience you have had with service at a restaurant, hotel, store, and so on.

3. Describe a very bad experience you have had with service somewhere.

People Say . . .

> *The customer is always right.* —Saying
>
> *You get what you pay for.* —Saying

What do these sayings mean?

Do you know of similar sayings?

Vocabulary Review

1. I told Kelly I would go to her party, but I was sick, so I _____ staying home.

2. Eric works at a restaurant. Last night, a customer left him a very big _____ , so Eric was happy.

3. If you go to a restaurant with one friend, you will have a _____ of two.

4. I didn't know what to order, so I asked the _____ to recommend something.

5. The first half of the exam was easy, but I _____ a lot of problems on the second half.

Answer box

Activity 2

Tipping in Various Situations

1. tip   6. tip

2. tip or don't tip   7. tip

3. don't tip   8. tip

4. tip   9. don't tip

5. don't tip   10. don't tip

Planes **or** Trains?

Starting Off

1. How do people usually travel?

2. How is transportation different in various countries?

3. How has transportation changed in recent years?

4. How do you think it will change in the future?

Vocabulary

alternative—(noun) choice, option

I might buy a new car with that money. My other **alternative** is to spend it on a vacation.

We have two **alternatives.** We could go to the movies or go out to dinner.

turbulence—(noun) lack of peace or smoothness

The plane bounced up and down like a basketball, because the **turbulence** was so great.

There was a lot of **turbulence** between the two countries. Finally, they went to war.

encounter—(verb) meet, experience

I love traveling, because I like to **encounter** new people.

The ship **encountered** a terrible storm and had to turn back.

convenience—(noun) something that is added to make one's life easier or more comfortable

Roger lives in a simple house. He has a refrigerator and a phone, but few other **conveniences.**

Computers, cell phones, and other modern **conveniences** allow people to stay in touch more easily.

The school has many **amenities,** such as a computer lab, a pool, and a gym.

enhance—(verb) improve, add to

Natalie **enhanced** her understanding of Brazilian culture by living in Brazil for a year.

The flowers **enhanced** the beauty of the room.

Reading

Every year, millions of people travel millions of miles, and they travel in various ways. Of course, two of the most popular **alternatives** are planes and trains. People may choose air travel because of its speed. However, a plane might not reach its destination much faster than a train. Airports are sometimes far from the city center, but train stations are more likely to be downtown. Therefore, getting to and from the airport can easily add a couple of hours and several dollars to your travel time.

▶ ▶ ▶ ▶ ▶ ▶ ▶ ▶

There's also the issue of comfort. On a plane, the seats are narrow, and there isn't much room to stretch your legs. **Turbulence** is another reason why planes can be uncomfortable. When a plane **encounters** turbulence, it seems as if the plane is jumping up and down. A train offers a smoother ride. Train passengers also have more freedom to get up and walk around. Airline passengers must stay in their seats during takeoff and landing, for example, and when there is turbulence. Trains do, however, lack certain **conveniences** available on planes, such as headphones, which allow passengers to listen to music. In the future, planes and trains may be **enhanced,** or new forms of transportation may be developed. For now, though, there may be no perfect way to travel.

Comprehension Questions

1. What are two main issues people consider when deciding between planes and trains?

2. What are some differences between planes and trains connected with the first issue?

3. What are some differences connected to the second issue?

4. How might transportation change in the future?

Discussion Activities

Activity 1

In a small group, discuss the advantages and disadvantages of planes and of trains. Try to think of ones that weren't described in the reading. Write your answers in the chart that follows.

Advantages of Planes	Disadvantages of Planes
Advantages of Trains	**Disadvantages of Trains**

Imagine that your class is taking a trip together. Your teacher will tell you the destination, which can be reached by plane or train. The class will form two groups and debate. Group A will try to convince the teacher that traveling by plane is a better alternative. Group B will argue for traveling by train. During the discussion, make sure that *everyone* has a chance to speak.

Conversation Tip

When you want to show that you disagree with someone, you can use these expressions:

That's not what I think.

That's not the way I see it.

A: I hate to take the train. It's so slow.

B: **That's not the way I see it.** I think taking the train is very relaxing and can give you great views.

Language Learning Tip

When you don't understand what someone said, you can use this expression:

Could you repeat that?

A: There was so much turbulence on my flight last week.

B: **Could you repeat that?**

A: There was a lot of turbulence. The flight wasn't smooth at all.

Try to use these tips in your discussion.

Wrap Up

Which group was more convincing?

What were the strengths and weaknesses of each group's presentation?

Activity 2

Working in a small group, choose one form of transportation (it doesn't have to be plane or train) and imagine that you are making a commercial to attract new passengers to it. Discuss possible ideas for the commercial. Choose one idea, then write a script for the commercial and perform it for the class. Or you might make a videotape of your commercial and show it to your classmates.

Activity 3

Work with a partner. Imagine that you have been given a pair of around-the-world plane tickets. Your tickets are good for six months, and you can stop at 10 destinations during that time. Your flights must always proceed in the same direction around the world, however. Plan the trip with your partner. What 10 places will you visit, and what will you do there? Write your answers here, then discuss them with the class.

Where We Will Go	What We Will Do
1.	1.
2.	2.
3.	3.
4.	4.
5.	5.
6.	6.
7.	7.
8.	8.
9.	9.
10.	10.

Write about It

1. What is your least favorite way to travel? Why?

2. Describe a travel experience that you have had.

3. Imagine that it is 100 years in the future. Describe an imaginary travel experience.

People Say . . .

To travel hopefully is a better thing than to arrive.
—Robert Louis Stevenson, Scottish writer

The world may be known without leaving the house.
—Lao Tzu, Chinese philosopher

What do these sayings mean?

Do you know of similar sayings?

Vocabulary Review

1. I've been to Africa, but I've never _____ an elephant.

2. The hotel room had a coffeemaker, a television, and some other

   _____ .

3. Chris didn't want to walk to work, but there was no other _____ .

   His car wasn't working, and the bus didn't run near his house.

4. I was eating lunch when the plane hit some _____ . Suddenly, my

   food fell into my lap.

5. You should add some salt. It will _____ the flavor of the soup.

28

Libraries **or** Bookstores?

Starting Off

1. How often do you go to the library?

2. How often do you go to the bookstore?

3. What is the last book you bought?

4. What kinds of things can people do at the library?

Vocabulary

establish—(verb) set up permanently

The business was **established** in 1978.

The country **established** a new government after the president died.

fine—(noun) money paid as a punishment

We returned the library books late, so we had to pay a ten-dollar **fine.**

Oliver was nervous about parking in the unmarked space, because he didn't want to get a **fine**.

promote—(verb) make publicity for, elevate, encourage

They wanted to **promote** the use of computers in the classroom.

The head of the company plans to **promote** five people to managerial positions.

literacy—(noun) ability to read and write

The president of the country wanted to increase the **literacy** rate of the people.

Teachers must learn about **literacy** if they want to teach in a primary school.

browse—(verb) look around

Henry spends his free time **browsing** the bookstore to see what new books there are.

Sarah takes a long time when she goes shopping because she likes to **browse** first.

Reading

Can you get anything for free in this world? If you go to a public library in the United States, you don't have to spend a dime. The Boston Public Library was **established** in 1848 and was the first public library to allow its patrons to borrow books. Now, most public libraries are furnished with books, videos, and CDs. Libraries usually allow people to take out items for a few weeks or until they are due. If the item is returned late, there may be a **fine.** Furthermore, many of the libraries are set up with computers that are connected to the Internet. Many libraries have a wide variety of classes to **promote literacy** for people of all ages. All you need to have to use a library's services is a library card.

▷ ▷ ▷ ▷ ▷ ▷ ▷ ▷

No matter what city you are in, you can find a bookstore. Some bookstores are big chain stores, and other bookstores are independent, catering to a particular niche. Bookstores are different from libraries in that once you buy a book, you own it. You do not have to worry about returning it by the due date. If you do not want to spend a lot of money, you could go to a used bookstore. Some bookstores are trying to attract as many customers as possible, so they sometimes offer refreshments, such as coffee or snacks, or evening entertainment. People who visit bookstores tend to **browse** the store until something looks appealing. When a customer purchases a book, he or she usually leaves the store with a big smile.

Comprehension Questions

1. When was the Boston Public Library established?

2. In addition to books, what else could you find at a public library?

3. List three different kinds of bookstores you might find in a city.

4. What do some bookstores do to attract customers?

Discussion Activities

Activity 1

In a small group, discuss the advantages and disadvantages of bookstores and of libraries. Try to think of things that weren't described in the reading. Write your answers in the chart that follows.

Advantages of Going to the Library	Disadvantages of Going to the Library
Advantages of Going to the Bookstore	Disadvantages of Going to the Bookstore

Because it is Saturday, George and Janice have the whole day off. They are excited about all of the free time they have. They can't decide if they should spend their time at the bookstore or at the library. The class will form two groups and debate. Group A will try to convince them that they should go to the bookstore. Group B will try to convince them that they should spend the day at the library. Make sure everyone has a chance to participate in the conversation.

Conversation Tip

When you want to ask for more information, you can use these expressions:

Could you give me an example?

Could you be more specific?

A: Libraries offer a lot more than bookstores.

B: **Could you give me an example?**

A: Libraries have not only books but DVDs, CDs, videos, and a lot of other things. Some bookstores don't have all those things.

Language Learning Tip

When you don't understand a word, you can use this expression:

What's the definition of _____ ?

A: The librarian said we would have to pay a fine if we return our books late. **What's the definition of "fine"?**

B: It means "money paid as a punishment."

Try to use these tips in your discussion.

Wrap Up

Which group was more convincing?

What were the strengths and weaknesses of each group's presentation?

Activity 2

With a partner, create a role play between a child and a parent. The child wants to buy a new book at the bookstore, but the parent wants the child to borrow the book from the library. The parent thinks buying the book is too expensive, while the child thinks reading a book more than once is important to becoming a better reader. When you have practiced your role play, perform it in front of your classmates.

28 _____

With a partner, write a definition for and give an example of each type of book.

Type of Book	Definition	Example
Fiction	_____	_____
Nonfiction	_____	_____
Historical fiction	_____	_____
Science fiction	_____	_____
Romance	_____	_____
Poetry	_____	_____
Self-help	_____	_____
Mystery	_____	_____
Reference	_____	_____
Humor	_____	_____
How-to	_____	_____
Biography	_____	_____
Autobiography	_____	_____

Now that you have clear definitions, answer the following questions with your partner. Be prepared to share your answers with the class.

What was one of your favorite books when you were a child?

Me: title: _____   My partner: title: _____

        type: _____   type: _____

What was one book that everyone in your high school had to read?

Me: title: _____   My partner: title: _____

        type: _____   type: _____

What is one of the worst books that you have ever read?

Me: title: _____   My partner: title: _____

          type: _____   type: _____

What is one book that has changed your life?

Me: title: _____   My partner: title: _____

          type: _____   type: _____

What is one book that you would like to read in the near future?

Me: title: _____   My partner: title: _____

          type: _____   type: _____

What is one book that you have in your house right now?

Me: title: _____   My partner: title: _____

          type: _____   type: _____

Imagine you were going to write your autobiography. What would the title of this book be?

Me: title: _____   My partner: title: _____

          type: _____   type: _____

Write about It

1. What was the first book you remember reading on your own? Describe your feelings about being able to read this book all by yourself.

2. When was the first time you went to the library?

3. What is your favorite bookstore? Why?

People Say . . .

> *Your library is your portrait.* —Holbrook Jackson, English writer

> *If a book is worth reading, it is worth buying.* —John Ruskin, English writer

What do these quotes mean?

Do you know of similar sayings?

Vocabulary Review

1. Before she buys shoes she likes to _____ the store to see all of the new styles.

2. The small island wanted to increase _____ rates among the teenage population.

3. Paul drove too fast on the highway, so the police officer stopped him and gave him a _____ of fifty dollars.

4. The school district wants to _____ an antismoking campaign at every grade level.

5. The famous clothing store was _____ in 1969.

Alike or Different?

Starting Off

1. Describe someone (a family member, friend, etc.) whose personality is similar to yours.

2. Describe someone whose personality is very different from yours.

3. What do you think is the best quality for a person to have?

4. What do you think is the worst quality for a person to have?

Vocabulary

spouse—(noun) husband or wife

Nick was Holly's boyfriend for two years. Now he's her **spouse.**

I'm single, but my brother has a **spouse.** They've been married since June.

trait—(noun) quality, characteristic

My roommate is kind, intelligent, and funny. She has many good **traits.**

Honesty is one of the most important **traits** for a friend to have.

hang around—(phrasal verb) spend time together

I used to **hang around** with Greg during high school, but then he moved away.

If you **hang around** with Americans all day, your English will improve.

precisely—(adverb) exactly

My mother told me to come home at **precisely** six o'clock, not before or after.

This school has the best English department in the country. That's **precisely** why I decided to study here.

stimulating—(adjective) exciting, giving one energy, causing one to become interested

That was a very **stimulating** lecture about modern art. Now I really want to go to the museum.

Our walk around the lake was very **stimulating.** I don't feel tired at all anymore.

Reading

No one else in the world is exactly like you. However, you probably know many people who are very similar to you. Some of them may be your family members, your closest friends, or even your **spouse.** You may enjoy spending time together and get along well because you share similar interests and personality **traits.** If you are a very calm person, for example, you might like to **hang around** with other calm people. You might not want to spend your time with energetic people who often argue. If you like to plan everything in advance, you may have problems with someone who always decides things at the last minute.

▷ ▷ ▷ ▷ ▷ ▷ ▷

However, some people are attracted to others **precisely** because of their differences. A very energetic person might enjoy spending time with someone calm as a chance to relax. The calm person, by contrast, might find it **stimulating** to be around someone who is more energetic. When people are different, they may reach a happy balance together. Which is a better match, people who are the same or people who are different? There doesn't seem to be any definite rule. Both kinds of matches can work. It depends on the people involved.

Comprehension Questions

1. List three examples of people you know who might be like you.

2. Why might a calm person not want to be with an energetic person?

3. Why might a calm person get along well with an energetic person?

4. Why might two very different people get along well together?

Discussion Activities

Activity 1

In a small group, talk about the advantages and disadvantages of being with someone like yourself and of being with someone very different. Write your answers in the chart that follows.

Advantages of Being Alike	Disadvantages of Being Alike

Advantages of Being Different	Disadvantages of Being Different

Hannah has been dating two guys, Walt and Vin. Now she is ready to have a more serious relationship and wants to date only one of them. The problem is that she can't decide which one to choose. She likes both of them very much, but they are very different. Walt is very much like Hannah. He is basically a quiet person. He has a few good friends but likes spending a lot of time with Hannah. Vin is more outgoing and independent. He likes being with Hannah, too, but he also enjoys spending a lot of time with his male friends. The class will form two groups and debate. Group A will try to convince Hannah to choose Walt. Group B will try to convince her to pick Vin. During this discussion, make sure that everyone has a chance to speak.

Conversation Tip

When you want to give someone more information, you can use these expressions:

> **In other words, . . .**

> **What I'm trying to say is . . .**

A: I think it's much easier to get along with someone who's similar to you.

B: Do you think that people who are different can't get along?

A: No. **What I'm trying to say is** that they can get along, but it's more difficult to do so.

Language Learning Tip

When you see a word and you don't know how to say it, you can use this expression:

> **How do you say** _____ **?**

A: I have to write down some information for the office at my language school. **How do you say** this word?

B: That's "spouse." It means your husband or wife.

Try to use these tips in your discussion.

Wrap Up

Which group was more convincing?

What were the strengths and weaknesses of each group's presentation?

Activity 2

Work with a partner. Ask him or her one question for each example in the list that follows; if the example read, "a. spend money b. save money," you would ask, "Do you spend money, or do you save money?" After your partner answers, circle *a* or *b,* depending on the answer. When you have asked all of your questions, your partner should ask you the same questions. Finally, count up the number of similar answers. Compare your results with those of other pairs. Which partners are the most similar? Which are the most different?

1. a. are calm   b. are emotional

2. a. plan ahead   b. do things at the last minute

3. a. are usually on time   b. are usually late

4. a. like being alone   b. dislike being alone

5. a. make decisions easily   b. have a hard time making decisions

6. a. ask others for advice   b. try to solve your problems by yourself

7. a. say exactly what you're thinking b. are careful about what you say

8. a. return phone calls   b. forget to return phone calls

9. a. borrow things from friends   b. avoid borrowing things from friends

10. a. lend things to friends   b. avoid lending things to friends

Activity 3

In a small group, talk about the four men and four women described in the text that follows. If you had to match each man with one woman, what matches would you make? Discuss your ideas with the class.

The Men

1. **Sam** is a doctor. On weekends, he likes to go see his favorite sports teams play. He also loves to travel. Sam is an independent person. He enjoys being with friends. However, he also likes spending time alone.

2. **Billy** works in a video store. He is very kind and is a little shy. Billy loves to paint. He hopes to be an artist one day, but most people do not want to buy his paintings.

3. **Ken** is a businessman. He is friendly and outgoing. He loves having a good discussion, but he sometimes gets upset when people disagree with him.

4. **Ned** is a scientist. Everyone says that one day he might become famous for his work. He never pays attention to his hair or clothes. He cares more about science than he does about looks or fashion. Ned doesn't like to spend money on fancy things. He buys only used cars and lives in a small apartment.

The Women

1. **Charlene** is a professor of art history. She recently wrote a book about Michelangelo. She spends a lot of time reading alone and is rather shy. Every year, she goes to Italy to visit museums and buy new clothes.

2. **Robin** works in a music store during the week and plays in a rock band on weekends. She is outgoing and has a lot of friends. She also has very strong opinions and tells people exactly what she thinks.

3. **Stella** leads camping trips in the mountains. She is full of energy and loves being with people. She enjoys playing all kinds of sports.

4. **Karen** is a very successful lawyer. She works long hours and likes to spend her free time relaxing at home. She especially enjoys watching old movies, alone or with a friend. Karen loves good food and fine wine.

Your Matches

1. _____ and _____

2. _____ and _____

3. _____ and _____

4. _____ and _____

Write about It

Describe the relationship between you and another person. Are you similar or different?

What makes a relationship between two people successful?

What kind of differences can cause the biggest problems in a relationship?

People Say . . .

Birds of a feather flock together. —Saying

Opposites attract. —Saying

What do these sayings mean?

Do you know of similar sayings?

Vocabulary Review

1. My job is very _____ . I'm always learning new things and meeting new people.

2. My _____ knows me better than anyone else in the world.

3. Bingo is very intelligent. He also has other _____ that are important in a dog.

4. During high school, Bev and Kim _____ together. They were best

friends.

5. When Will bakes, he measures everything _____ . He doesn't want to

have too much or too little of anything.

Phone **or** Email?

Starting Off

1. How do you keep in touch with your friends and family?

2. About how much time do you spend on the phone each day?

3. About how much time do you spend communicating by email each week?

4. How has communication changed in the last few years?

Vocabulary

remarkable—(adjective) surprising, amazing

> I can't believe how much Stefano's English has improved. The change is **remarkable.**

> Ralph eats a **remarkable** amount. I've never seen anyone eat so much.

drastically—(adverb) very much, severely

> The restaurant increased its prices **drastically.** I can't afford to go there anymore.

> It wasn't very cold yesterday morning. Then the temperature dropped **drastically,** and it started to snow.

simultaneously—(adverb) happening together, at the same time

> Yoko likes to watch the news in English, so that she can learn about the world and practice her listening skill **simultaneously.**

> My friend is dating four guys **simultaneously.** I think one should be enough.

ultimate—(adjective) top, final

> You'll love Hawaii. A trip there is the **ultimate** vacation.

> Skiing is the **ultimate** sport. It's fast, exciting, and great exercise.

respect—(noun) way, manner

> Kate resembles her mother in many **respects.** Both of them are kind, smart, and funny.

> I like my new job, but my old one was better in some **respects.** For one thing, I got more vacation time.

Reading

Of all the technical advances in modern times, some of the most **remarkable** have been in communications. For hundreds of years, people who lived far apart communicated by letter. Communication changed **drastically** when Alexander Graham Bell invented the telephone in 1876. One day, Bell spilled acid on his clothes and called to his assistant for help. He said, "Mr. Watson, come here. I want you." Those were the first words spoken over a telephone. The telephone allowed people to contact each other immediately and to communicate **simultaneously.** It was no longer necessary to wait days, weeks, or even months for a written response. The telephone seemed to be the **ultimate** form of communications technology.

▷▷▷▷▷▷▷

When computer technology arrived, the world of communications changed yet again. One very important step took place in 1969 when the United States government's Advanced Research Project Agency developed the ARPANET, a network that connected computers at various universities and research centers. This type of technology led to the Internet, and now email has become one of the main ways that people keep in touch. In many **respects,** writing an email message is the same as writing a letter. However, email is fast, like the telephone. What kind of inventions will we see in the future? No one knows—yet.

Comprehension Questions

1. What was the reason for the first telephone conversation?

2. What are two advantages of the telephone over letters?

3. What was the ARPANET?

4. How did the Internet change people's lives?

Discussion Activities

Activity 1

In a small group, discuss the advantages and disadvantages of the telephone and of email. Write your answers in the chart that follows.

Advantages of the Telephone	Disadvantages of the Telephone
Advantages of Email	Disadvantages of Email

Ramon is going to study abroad in the United States for a semester. He has a choice between two homestay situations. Both seem very good, but there is one difference. The first family doesn't want him to use their phone or to have a phone installed in his room. Using a cell phone at the house is not an option, because the reception there is very bad. The family will, however, let him use their computer for email. They don't use the computer much, so he will be able to use it whenever he wants. The second family will let Ramon use their phone whenever he wants, but they don't have a computer. Ramon doesn't have a computer either, and he can't afford to buy one. The class will form two groups and debate. Group A will try to convince Ramon to live with the first family. Group B will try to convince Ramon to live with the second family. During this discussion, make sure that everyone has a chance to speak.

Conversation Tip

When you want to disagree and add your own opinion, you can use these expressions:

I see what you mean, but . . .

That's a good point, but . . .

A: For me, using email is better than using the phone, because with email I can plan out what I want to say.

B: **I see what you mean, but** sometimes it's nice to hear the other person's voice.

Language Learning Tip

If you don't understand what people say because they speak too quickly, you can use this expression:

A: The email system isn't working now. I don't know what's wrong with it.

B: **Would you mind saying that again more slowly?**

A: The email system isn't working now. There's some problem.

Try to use these tips in your discussion.

Wrap Up

Which group was more convincing?

What were the strengths and weaknesses of each group's presentation?

Activity 2

In a small group, prepare a proposal for increasing your school's Internet and email capabilities. Where should there be new computer access? How will it help students? Why should the school spend money on it? Share your proposal with your classmates. Which proposal is the most convincing?

Activity 3

In the United States, there is a game called "telephone," which is for a group of people. In this game, one person says a sentence to another person, and that person repeats the sentence to a third person. This continues until the last person in the group hears the sentence and tries to repeat it. Each person must whisper the sentence into the next person's ear, so that no one else can hear what he or she is saying. The person who is listening can only hear the sentence once. He or she cannot ask the speaker to repeat it and cannot ask whether he or she has understood the sentence correctly. By the time the sentence reaches the last person, it has often changed, and that's what makes the game so interesting.

To play this game, the class will split into two teams. Your teacher will give the first person in each team a sentence. (Examples for the teacher are in the answer key.) The first person will repeat the sentence to the second person in the team, and the game will continue this way until the last person in each team has heard the sentence. Finally, the last person in each team will write the sentence on the board. If a team gets the sentence exactly right, it gets one point.

Write about It

1. Write a message to a friend or family member about the interesting things now happening in your life.

2. Pretend you are an American studying abroad in another country. Write a message to a friend or family member.

3. How will communication be different in the future?

People Say . . .

I do not fear computers, I fear the lack of them.
—Isaac Asimov, American science fiction writer

The unsaid part is the best of every discourse.
—Ralph Waldo Emerson, American essayist and poet

What do these sayings mean?

Do you know of similar sayings?

Vocabulary Review

1. Have you ever visited Australia? The beauty of the beaches there is

   _____ .

2. I studied French and Spanish _____ during college. It was difficult, because I was always confusing the two languages.

3. New York is very exciting, but I don't like it in some _____ . For example, it's too crowded and expensive.

4. Ed looks _____ different now. He's lost a lot of weight and has much longer hair. I didn't even know who he was at first.

5. Frank has had many different jobs in the company, and one day he would like to be the company's president. That would be the _____ job for him.

Appendix: Vocabulary

accommodations—(noun) a room in a hotel or other place where you stay while on vacation (7)

accomplish—(verb) do something important, reach a goal (16)

acquaintance—(noun) someone you know, but who is not a close friend (4)

acquire—(verb) get (17)

allow—(verb) let something happen (13)

alternative—(noun) choice, option (27)

anonymous—(adjective) unknown, not connected to a name (2)

audience—(noun) people who watch or listen to a performance or movie (2)

autograph—(noun) a famous person's written name (2)

average—(adjective) not unusually big or small (7)

bankruptcy—(noun) the state of not being able to pay your debts (23)

benefits—(noun) money or advantages from a job (13)

book—(verb) arrange—with a hotel, restaurant, theater, etc., to go there at a particular time in the future (19)

bound—(adjective) expected (8)

browse—(verb) look around (28)

cancel—(verb) end an agreement that exists (23)

clerk—(noun) a person who works in a store and helps customers (3)

clutter—(noun) a lot of things that are scattered in a messy way (17)

committed—(adjective) willing to work hard at something (15)

compare—(verb) look at two or more things to see how they are similar or different (3)

compatible—(adjective) fitting together or matching well (18)

complain—(verb) say that you are unhappy about someone or something (13)

condominium—(noun) a building that consists of separate units, each of which is owned by the people living in it (25)

conduct—(verb) do something to get information or to prove a fact (21)

consumer—(noun) a person who buys things (1)

convenience—(noun) something that is added to make one's life easier or more comfortable (27)

cover—(verb) report on, have information about (20)

customer—(noun) a person who pays for a service or item (3)

debt—(noun) the amount of money you owe (23)

destination—(noun) the place that someone or something is going to (19)

determine—(verb) decide something, influence an outcome (16)

devote—(verb) use for a special purpose, give one's time and energy (22)

diabetes—(noun) a disease in which there is too much sugar in the blood (15)

dilemma—(noun) problem, difficult situation (22)

discard—(verb) get rid of something (17)

dominant—(adjective) stronger and more important than other people or things (12)

drastically—(adverb) very much, severely (30)

drowsy—(adjective) tired, sleepy (16)

elope—(verb) go away secretly with someone to get married (7)

emigrate—(verb) leave one's country to live permanently in another country (11)

enable—(verb) allow, make something possible (20)

encompass—(verb) include (14)

encounter—(verb) meet, experience (27)

enhance—(verb) improve, add to (27)

envision—(verb) imagine something, especially as a future possibility (5)

escape—(verb) get away from a place or a dangerous situation (5)

establish—(verb) set up permanently (28)

ethical—(adjective) morally good or bad (15)

exotic—(adjective) unusual and exciting because of a connection with a foreign country (7)

extremely—(adverb) very, really (4)

fade—(verb) become weaker (4)

fiction—(noun) something that is not true, an untrue story (14)

fine—(noun) money paid as a punishment (28)

flexibility—(noun) room for freedom   (14)

folks—(noun) people, parents   (24)

follow—(verb) pay attention to   (2)

fond—(adjective) liking someone or something very much   (21)

generate—(verb) produce or make something   (9)

gratuity—(noun)—tip, money (beyond a fee) that you give someone for a service   (26)

groom—(verb) take care of one's appearance   (21)

hang around—(phrasal verb) spend time together   (29)

hectic—(adjective) busy, rushed   (1)

hemisphere—(noun) one of the two hemispheres of your brain, one of the halves of the earth   (12)

holistic—(adjective) reflecting the idea that a person or a thing needs to be treated as a whole   (12)

honor—(verb) treat with special respect   (11)

hostile—(adjective) aggressive, easily angered   (6)

huge—(adjective) very big   (9)

ideal—(adjective) perfect   (8)

illusion—(noun) something that may seem real but actually is not   (18)

imagination—(noun) the ability to form pictures and ideas in your mind   (12)

impressive—(adjective) admirable because of being very good, large, important, and so on   (9)

incredibly—(adverb) to a very great degree   (5)

industrialized—(adjective) developed, advanced, with many factories   (10)

ingredients—(noun) types of food needed to make a particular dish   (1)

institute—(verb) start, begin to use   (22)

interaction—(noun) the activity of talking to other people, working with them, and so on   (3)

investment—(noun) the money people put into a company, business, or bank to make a profit   (25)

labor—(noun) physical work   (10)

laid-back—(adjective) relaxed, not worried   (6)

landlord—(noun) a person who rents a room, apartment, or building to someone else   (25)

legend—(noun) an old well-known story   (11)

lifetime—(noun) the time one is alive, the number of years one lives   (4)

link—(noun) connection, relation   (6)

literacy—(noun) ability to read and write   (28)

logical—(adjective) reasonable   (12)

lonely—(adjective) feeling sad because you are alone   (19)

luxury—(noun) comfort, especially because of having expensive things   (24)

mobility—(noun) the ability to move easily from one place to another   (25)

momentarily—(adverb) for a short time   (14)

morale—(noun) level of confidence and positive feelings, usually among a group   (21)

mortgage—(noun) a legal arrangement with a bank, in which a person borrows money (usually for a house) and pays it back over a number of years   (25)

navigate—(verb) find the way to or through a place   (3)

obesity—(noun) the condition of being too fat to an extent that poses a health risk   (15)

obscure—(adjective) little known, hard to understand   (14)

obstacle—(noun) something that prevents you from moving forward or accomplishing a goal   (6)

obvious—(adjective) easy to see, easy to know   (10)

off—(adjective) free, without work   (10)

otherwise—(adverb) if not, in another situation   (4)

outdated—(adjective) not useful or modern anymore   (17)

pamper—(verb) give someone a lot of attention or things, often too much or too many   (24)

party—(noun) group, especially in a restaurant   (26)

perk—(noun) something you get (usually from a job) in addition to what is expected   (23)

perspective—(noun) point of view, opinion   (20)

picture—(verb) imagine, see in one's mind   (8)

policy—(noun) rule, idea about a certain issue   (22)

precisely—(adverb) exactly   (29)

promote—(verb) make publicity for, elevate, encourage   (28)

purchase—(verb) buy   (23)

reception—(noun) a large formal party to celebrate an event or to welcome someone   (7)

recognize—(verb) see someone's face and know who that person is   (2)

relative—(noun) a member of your family   (5)

remarkable—(adjective) surprising, amazing   (30)

respect—(noun) way, manner   (30)

retailer—(noun) a person who sells things   (1)

rough it—(phrasal verb) live without comforts   (24)

roughly—(adverb) about, nearly   (10)

run into—(phrasal verb) meet or experience accidentally   (26)

rural—(adjective) related to small towns   (8)

salary—(noun) the amount of money one makes from working   (13)

sedentary—(adjective) not moving or exercising very much   (15)

self-sufficient—(adjective) independent, able to do things by oneself   (24)

sensible—(adjective) using thought, not emotion   (18)

sentimental—(adjective) based on feelings rather than practical reasons   (17)

server—(noun) waiter or waitress, someone who serves food at a restaurant   (26)

shift—(noun) required working time (usually eight hours)   (16)

simultaneously—(adverb) happening together, at the same time   (30)

skeptical—(adjective) not believing things easily   (18)

solitary—(adjective) alone, away from others   (16)

spouse—(noun) husband or wife   (29)

still—(adjective) not moving   (20)

stimulating—(adjective) exciting, giving one energy, causing one to become interested   (29)

stranger—(noun) a person whom you do not know   (19)

strive—(verb) try very hard to do something difficult   (6)

suit—(verb) be acceptable or convenient for a particular person   (9)

survey—(verb) ask many people the same set of questions to collect information   (18)

temperature—(noun) the measure of how hot or cold a place or thing is   (5)

tolerate—(verb) be able to accept something unpleasant or difficult   (21)

tradition—(noun) a belief, custom, or way of doing something that has existed for a long time   (11)

trailer—(noun) an advertisement for a new movie that shows clips from it   (9)

trait—(noun) quality, characteristic   (29)

transportation—(noun) a method of carrying passengers or goods from one place to another (19)

trend—(noun) the way a situation is changing or developing (1)

turbulence—(noun) lack of peace or smoothness (27)

ultimate—(adjective) top, final (30)

universally—(adverb) completely, widely (22)

update—(noun) new information (20)

urban—(adjective) related to cities (8)

version—(noun) a copy of something that is slightly different from other forms of it (11)

wind up—(phrasal verb) finally do something, finally become (26)

worry—(verb) be anxious or unhappy about something (13)

Answer Key

Chapter 1
Dining In or Eating Out?

Comprehension Questions
1. 4.2 meals per week
2. 3.8 meals per week
3. more than 8 percent
4. banking, shoe repair, dry cleaning, filling prescriptions

Vocabulary Review
1. ingredients
2. trend
3. consumers
4. hectic
5. retailers

Chapter 2
Famous or Anonymous?

Comprehension Questions
1. have a hit song
2. win an Olympic medal
3. appear in commercials
4. The person could be recognized and asked for an autograph.

Vocabulary Review
1. follow
2. anonymous
3. autograph
4. recognize
5. audience

Chapter 3
Going to the Store or Shopping over the Internet?

Comprehension Questions
1. 47.6 billion
2. People are comfortable using the computer, and information is encrypted.
3. a few
4. They like to touch items, test items, and have social interaction with others.

Vocabulary Review
1. clerks
2. compare
3. customers
4. navigate
5. interactions

Chapter 4
Friends or Acquaintances?

Comprehension Questions
1. life, death, love, dreams
2. One friend has a problem.
3. work, vacation, family
4. It may become stronger or fade over time.

Vocabulary Review
1. lifetime
2. otherwise
3. extremely
4. acquaintance
5. faded

Chapter 5
Summer or Winter?

Comprehension Questions
1. around June 21
2. visiting relatives or going to summer camp
3. around December 21
4. skiing and snowboarding

Vocabulary Review
1. incredibly
2. relatives
3. envisioned
4. escape
5. temperature

Chapter 6
Type A or Type B?

Comprehension Questions
1. competitive, concerned with time, in a hurry
2. laid-back, patient
3. Yes, the women are less hostile.
4. No.

Vocabulary Review
1. link
2. hostile
3. obstacle
4. strives
5. laid-back

Chapter 7
Having a Big Wedding or Eloping?

Comprehension Questions
1. about $20,000
2. bride, groom, parents, bridesmaids, and best man
3. about $5,000
4. Eloping is cheaper and unconventional.

Vocabulary Review
1. accommodations
2. exotic
3. elope
4. reception
5. average

Chapter 8
Big City or Small Town?

Comprehension Questions
1. restaurants, movies, art, music
2. There is good public transportation.
3. The pace of life is slower.
4. They see the same faces every day.

Vocabulary Review
1. bound
2. urban
3. ideal
4. rural
5. picture

Chapter 9
Video at Home or Movie at the Theater?

Comprehension Questions
1. $8.4 billion
2. trailers, high-quality sound, stadium seating, and huge screens
3. 96 percent
4. $21.5 billion

Vocabulary Review
1. generate
2. huge
3. trailers
4. impressive
5. suits

Chapter 10
Time or Money?

Comprehension Questions
1. the United States, Australia, Canada, Japan, Mexico, Brazil, Great Britain, Germany
2. Canadians
3. Germans have about 10 weeks more time off.
4. No.

Vocabulary Review
1. roughly
2. off
3. obvious
4. labor
5. industrialized

Chapter 11
Bagels or Doughnuts?

Comprehension Questions
1. women in Poland who were giving birth
2. King Sobreski saved Vienna from Turkish invaders.
3. Holland
4. The Pilgrims brought it with them in the 1600s.

Vocabulary Review
1. emigrated
2. honor
3. legend
4. versions
5. tradition

Chapter 12
Left-Brain Person or Right-Brain Person?

Comprehension Questions
1. two
2. right-hand movement, spoken and written language, number skills, and scientific language
3. left-hand movement, imagination, spatial relations, and music and art awareness
4. the violin

Vocabulary Review
1. holistic
2. imagination
3. dominant
4. logical
5. hemisphere

Chapter 13
Working for a Small Company or Being Self-Employed?

Comprehension Questions
1. They set their own hours.
2. not always
3. The worker will be compensated.
4. health insurance and a retirement plan

Vocabulary Review
1. salary
2. complain
3. benefits
4. allows
5. worries

Chapter 14
Fiction or Nonfiction?

Comprehension Questions
1. Fiction writing doesn't have to be real, so fiction writers can make up anything.
2. Fiction can help readers escape everyday life and experience a world of excitement.
3. history, biography, politics, science
4. to learn something

Vocabulary Review
1. encompasses
2. obscure
3. fiction
4. flexibility
5. momentarily

Chapter 15
Diet or Exercise?

Comprehension Questions
1. about 65 million
2. health concerns, issues with weight or appearance, and ethical or religious reasons
3. 60 percent
4. decreased risk of heart disease, diabetes, and obesity

Vocabulary Review
1. diabetes
2. sedentary
3. committed
4. ethical
5. obesity

Chapter 16
Early Bird or Night Owl?

Comprehension Questions
1. start work early, exercise
2. going to parties, solitary activities (reading, studying)
3. They might have to work.
4. A night owl might come home as an early bird is leaving.

Vocabulary Review
1. solitary
2. shifts
3. drowsy
4. determine
5. accomplish

Chapter 17
Pack Rat or Minimalist?

Comprehension Questions
1. someone who holds on to old stuff
2. They collect things as a hobby; items may be useful in the future; items have sentimental value.
3. someone who enjoys empty space more than stuff
4. Once you get something new, you get rid of something old.

Vocabulary Review
1. acquire
2. outdated
3. discarded
4. sentimental
5. clutter

Chapter 18
Love at First Sight or Love over Time?

Comprehension Questions
1. 37 percent
2. He or she looks at someone and gets the feeling that the two of them belong together.
3. Love takes much longer.
4. They get to know each other over time.

Vocabulary Review
1. illusion
2. compatible
3. surveyed
4. sensible
5. skeptical

Chapter 19
Group Tour or Independent Travel?

Comprehension Questions
1. go to a hotel that has already been booked
2. the tour operator
3. the person who is traveling
4. the independent traveler because he or she has to plan and do things alone

Vocabulary Review
1. strangers
2. booked
3. transportation
4. destination
5. lonely

Chapter 20
Newspaper or TV News?

Comprehension Questions
1. We can learn about news immediately. We can see news happening.
2. CNN broadcasts news 24 hours a day.
3. People can read about the news only after it has happened. They can only see still photos.
4. Newspaper stories might have more detail. You can go back and reread parts of an article.

Vocabulary Review
1. perspectives
2. still
3. enables
4. update
5. cover

Chapter 21
Cats or Dogs?

Comprehension Questions
1. 61 million
2. Morale and attendance improved.
3. 74 million
4. 30 percent

Vocabulary Review
1. tolerate
2. grooming
3. morale
4. fond
5. conducted

Chapter 22
Some English or All English?

Comprehension Questions
1. They make friends who speak the same language.
2. Students can't practice what they've learned in class, so their English doesn't improve quickly.
3. The schools have English-only policies.
4. They need time to speak their own language instead of struggling with English.

Vocabulary Review
1. universally
2. policy
3. dilemma
4. instituted
5. devotes

Chapter 23
Cash or Credit?

Comprehension Questions
1. 1.3 million
2. to avoid paying interest
3. airline miles or cash back
4. $8,500

Vocabulary Review
1. cancel
2. bankruptcy
3. purchase
4. perks
5. debt

Chapter 24
Living in Luxury or Roughing It?

Comprehension Questions
1. They work hard.
2. You don't have to cook and clean, and some hotels have special facilities.
3. It's cheaper. You can see how self-sufficient you can be.
4. You might start thinking about a hot shower and a warm bed.

Vocabulary Review
1. pampered
2. luxury
3. self-sufficient
4. rough it
5. folks

Chapter 25
Renting an Apartment or Buying a Condominium?

Comprehension Questions
1. a monthly mortgage, maintenance costs, and yearly taxes
2. call the landlord
3. A condominium owner is building equity each month and is not dependent on a landlord for maintenance issues.
4. The owner can sell it to make some money.

Vocabulary Review
1. landlord
2. investment
3. mortgage
4. condominium
5. mobility

Chapter 26
Tipping or No Tipping?

Comprehension Questions
1. when they travel abroad
2. 15–20 percent of the bill
3. when there is a large party
4. when they don't realize that the tip has been included in the bill

Vocabulary Review
1. wound up
2. gratuity
3. party
4. server
5. ran into

Chapter 27
Planes or Trains?

Comprehension Questions
1. speed and comfort
2. Planes are faster. Airports are farther from downtown than train stations.
3. Planes have narrow seats with little legroom, and they encounter turbulence. Passengers can get up and walk around more on trains. Planes have music.
4. Planes and trains may be enhanced. New forms of transportation may be developed.

Vocabulary Review
1. encountered
2. conveniences
3. alternative
4. turbulence
5. enhance

Chapter 28
Libraries or Bookstores?

Comprehension Questions
1. in 1848
2. videos, CDs, and computers
3. big chain, independent, and used
4. offer refreshments or entertainment

Vocabulary Review
1. browse
2. literacy
3. fine
4. promote
5. established

Chapter 29
Alike or Different?

Comprehension Questions
1. family members, friends, spouse
2. The energetic person might like to argue.
3. The calm person might find the energetic person stimulating.
4. They may reach a happy balance together.

Vocabulary Review
1. stimulating
2. spouse
3. traits
4. hung around
5. precisely

Chapter 30
Phone or Email?

Comprehension Questions
1. Alexander Graham Bell spilled acid on his clothes and needed help.
2. speed and simultaneous communication
3. a network developed by the U.S. government to connect computers at various universities and research centers
4. It made email one of the main ways that people keep in touch.

Activity 3
Sentences for the Telephone Game (Note that all sentences begin with a name.)
1. Alice read alone around eleven.
2. Bob bought a small bowl at the mall.
3. Leslie tried to grow her hair a little longer.
4. Barry felt very bad after eating the berries.

Vocabulary Review
1. remarkable
2. simultaneously
3. respects
4. drastically
5. ultimate

Perception